W9-AGA-974

Better Homes and Gardens®

COOKING

ITALIAN

Our seal assures you that every recipe in
Cooking Italian has been tested
in the Better Homes and Gardens®
Test Kitchen. This means that each recipe is
practical and reliable, and meets our
high standards of taste appeal.

© Copyright 1990 by Meredith Corporation, Des Moines, Iowa. All Rights Reserved. Printed in the United States of America.
First Edition. Printing Number and Year: 5 4   96 95 94
Library of Congress Catalog Card Number: 89-82437   ISBN: 0-696-01918-3

When I married into an Italian family, I discovered many wonders of Italian cooking. However, I found that preparing our favorites meant starting with fresh ingredients and cooking for long hours. This type of cooking and our on-the-go life-style didn't coincide. With our desire for Italian foods and fresh-cooked meals after work, I knew something would have to give.

Cooking Italian, it seemed to me, was my chance to help myself and others who enjoy preparing these foods, but who don't have hours to spend in the kitchen. To my surprise, I discovered many of the classics, such as *Fettuccine Alfredo* and *Italian-Style Pepper Steak,* are quick and easy to fix. As for other recipes that traditionally require more time, such as *Lasagna* and *Zuppa Inglese,* I found ways I could streamline and update them for today's cook.

Now, with these versions of the recipes, I can go home from work and have an Italian-approved meal on the table in minutes instead of hours. You can, too. Page through this book and discover traditional Italian as well as American-Italian recipes that meet the needs of your busy life-style.

Shelli McConnell

Editor
Cooking Italian

Tomatoey Tuna Sauce
(see recipe, page 6)
Breadsticks
(see recipe, page 84)

Crostata
(see recipe, page 116)

On the front cover:
Cheesy Manicotti
(see recipe, page 22)

Contents

PASTAS & SAUCES

To most people the essence of Italian cooking is pasta.

Whether sauce is spooned over, tossed with, or layered between it,

pasta is an all-time favorite. In this chapter, you'll

find classic Italian pasta dishes such as Fettuccine Alfredo and

Spaghetti and Meatballs plus new American-Italian pasta dishes such

as Fusilli and Vegetable Toss and Primavera Pasta Pie.

Fresh Tomato and Basil Sauce

For a delicious variation, omit the basil and stir in 3 tablespoons drained capers and 10 sliced pitted ripe olives.

¼ **cup finely chopped onion**
2 **cloves garlic, minced**
2 **tablespoons olive oil, margarine,**
   or **butter**

● In a medium saucepan cook onion and garlic in hot olive oil, margarine, or butter till onion is tender but not brown.

3 **pounds ripe fresh tomatoes, peeled,**
   seeded, and chopped (about 4 cups)
¼ **teaspoon salt**
¼ **teaspoon pepper**
¼ **cup snipped fresh basil**

● Carefully stir in the fresh tomatoes, salt, and pepper. Bring to boiling; reduce heat. Simmer, uncovered, for 35 to 40 minutes or to desired consistency. Stir in basil. Cook about 5 minutes more to blend flavors.

6 **ounces packaged capellini, spaghetti,**
   or **other pasta**

● Meanwhile, cook pasta (see chart, page 8). Immediately drain. Serve sauce over pasta. Makes 6 side-dish servings.

Nutrition information per serving: 173 calories, 5 g protein, 28 g carbohydrate, 5 g fat (1 g saturated), 0 mg cholesterol, 102 mg sodium, 277 mg potassium.

Pasta Smothered with Onions

A sumptuous side dish with a sweet, mellow flavor. (Pictured on page 40.)

2 **medium onions, cut into thin wedges**
   (2 cups)
1 **clove garlic, minced**
2 **tablespoons margarine** *or* **butter**

● In a covered, medium saucepan cook onions and garlic in margarine or butter over low heat about 20 minutes or till very tender, stirring occasionally. Uncover and cook over medium-high heat about 10 minutes more or till onions are a deep golden color, stirring frequently.

⅓ **cup chicken broth**
¼ **cup dry white wine**
⅛ **teaspoon pepper**

● Stir in the chicken broth, white wine, and pepper. Boil gently, uncovered, for 6 to 8 minutes or till most of the liquid is evaporated, stirring frequently.

4 **ounces packaged linguine, fettuccine,**
   or **other pasta**
¼ **cup shredded Bel Paese** *or* **Gruyère**
   cheese (1 ounce)
2 **tablespoons snipped parsley**

● Meanwhile, cook pasta (see chart, page 8). Immediately drain. Return pasta to saucepan. Add onion mixture. Add the cheese and parsley. Place saucepan over low heat. Toss till pasta is well coated and mixture is heated through. Transfer to a warm serving dish. Makes 4 side-dish servings.

Nutrition information per serving: 220 calories, 7 g protein, 26 g carbohydrate, 9 g fat (3 g saturated), 8 mg cholesterol, 159 mg sodium, 138 mg potassium.

Tomatoey Tuna Sauce

This home-style classic blends tomatoes, tuna, and pasta.

⅓ **cup finely chopped onion**
2 **cloves garlic, minced**
1 **tablespoon olive oil *or* cooking oil**

● In a large saucepan cook the onion and garlic in hot olive oil or cooking oil till onion is tender but not brown.

1 **28-ounce can tomatoes, finely cut up**
1 **6-ounce can tomato paste**
1 **3.5-ounce can pitted ripe olives, drained**
1 **teaspoon sugar**
¾ **teaspoon dried Italian seasoning, crushed**
⅛ **teaspoon salt**
⅛ **teaspoon ground red pepper**
1 **12½-ounce can tuna, drained and broken into chunks**

● Carefully stir in the *undrained* tomatoes, tomato paste, ripe olives, sugar, Italian seasoning, salt, and ground red pepper. Bring to boiling; reduce heat. Boil gently, uncovered, about 20 minutes or to desired consistency. Stir in tuna and heat through.

8 **ounces packaged mostaccioli, rigatoni, *or* other pasta**
1 **tablespoon snipped parsley**

● Meanwhile, cook pasta (see chart, page 8). Immediately drain. Return pasta to saucepan. Add sauce and toss gently till pasta is coated. Transfer to a warm serving dish. Sprinkle with parsley. Makes 4 main-dish servings.

Nutrition information per serving: 464 calories, 35 g protein, 63 g carbohydrate, 10 g fat (1 g saturated), 44 mg cholesterol, 860 mg sodium, 1,121 mg potassium.

Fusilli and Vegetable Toss

To transform this side dish into 2 main-dish servings, stir 1½ cups chopped cooked chicken into the mushroom mixture and heat through.

4 **ounces packaged fusilli, spaghetti, *or* other pasta**

● Cook pasta (see chart, page 8). Immediately drain. Return pasta to saucepan; keep warm.

2 **cups sliced fresh mushrooms**
⅓ **cup finely chopped onion**
1 **clove garlic, minced**
1 **tablespoon olive oil *or* cooking oil**
1 **medium zucchini, halved lengthwise and sliced ¼ inch thick**
½ **cup sun-dried tomatoes (oil pack), drained and chopped**
½ **teaspoon dried Italian seasoning, crushed**
Finely shredded Parmesan cheese (optional)

● Meanwhile, in a large skillet cook the mushrooms, onion, and garlic in hot olive oil or cooking oil over medium-high heat till vegetables are tender. Add zucchini, sun-dried tomatoes, and Italian seasoning. Cook and stir for 2 to 3 minutes more or till zucchini is crisp-tender. Add mushroom mixture to pasta. Toss gently till well mixed. Transfer to a warm serving dish. If desired, sprinkle with Parmesan cheese. Makes 4 side-dish servings.

Nutrition information per serving: 242 calories, 7 g protein, 39 g carbohydrate, 8 g fat (1 g saturated), 0 mg cholesterol, 26 mg sodium, 895 mg potassium.

Breadsticks
(see recipe, page 84)

Tomatoey Tuna Sauce

Cooking Pasta

In a large saucepan or Dutch oven, bring water (about 3 quarts of water for 4 to 8 ounces of pasta) to boiling. If desired, add 1 teaspoon salt and 1 tablespoon olive oil or cooking oil to help keep the pasta separated. Add pasta a little at a time so water does not stop boiling. (Hold long pasta, such as spaghetti, at one end and dip other end into water. As pasta softens, gently curl it around pan and down into water.) Reduce heat slightly. Boil, uncovered, for time specified or till pasta is al dente (tender but slightly firm). Stir occasionally. Test often for doneness near end of cooking time. Immediately drain in a colander.

In recipes that call for packaged pasta, you may substitute 8 ounces homemade pasta or fresh refrigerated pasta for 4 ounces of the packaged product.

Packaged Pasta	Cooking Time
Acini di pepe	5 to 6 minutes
Anelli	9 to 10 minutes
Capellini	5 to 6 minutes
Cavatelli	12 minutes
Conchiglie	12 to 14 minutes
Conchigliette	8 to 9 minutes
Conchiglioni	23 to 25 minutes
Farfalle	10 minutes
Fettuccine	8 to 10 minutes
Fusilli	15 minutes
Gemelli	10 minutes
Lasagna	10 to 12 minutes
Linguine	8 to 10 minutes
Mafalda	10 to 12 minutes
Manicotti	18 minutes
Mostaccioli or Penne	14 minutes
Orzo or Rosamarina	5 to 8 minutes
Rigatoni	15 minutes
Rotelle	8 to 10 minutes
Ruote	12 minutes
Spaghetti	10 to 12 minutes
Spaghettini	8 to 10 minutes
Tortellini	15 minutes
Tripolini	5 to 6 minutes
Vermicelli	5 to 7 minutes
Ziti	14 to 15 minutes

Fresh Homemade or Fresh Refrigerated Pasta	Cooking Time*
Farfalle	2 to 3 minutes
Fettuccine	1½ to 2 minutes
Lasagna	2 to 3 minutes
Linguine	1½ to 2 minutes
Ravioli	6 to 8 minutes
Tortellini	8 to 10 minutes
Tripolini	2 to 3 minutes

*If homemade pasta is dried or frozen, allow a few more minutes.

Homemade Pasta

2 cups all-purpose flour **½ teaspoon salt**	● In a large mixing bowl stir together the flour and the salt. Make a well in the center of the mixture.
2 beaten eggs **⅓ cup water** **1 teaspoon olive oil *or* cooking oil**	● In a small mixing bowl stir together the eggs, water, and olive oil or cooking oil. Add to the flour mixture and mix well.
⅓ cup all-purpose flour	● Sprinkle kneading surface with the flour. Turn dough out onto floured surface. Knead till dough is smooth and elastic (8 to 10 minutes total). Cover and let rest for 10 minutes.
	● Divide dough into fourths. On a lightly floured surface, roll *each* fourth into a 12-inch square. Let stand about 20 minutes or till slightly dry. Shape as desired (see tip, page 10). *Or*, if using a pasta machine, pass each fourth of dough through machine, according to manufacturer's directions, till 1/16 inch thick. Shape as desired. (See tip, page 10.)
	● Cook pasta (see chart, page 8), allowing a few more minutes for dried or frozen pasta. Drain well. Makes 1 pound fresh pasta.

Nutrition information per ounce: 69 calories, 2 g protein, 12 g carbohydrate, 1 g fat (0 g saturated), 27 mg cholesterol, 75 mg sodium, 15 mg potassium.

Herb Pasta **1 teaspoon dried basil, marjoram, *or* sage, crushed**	Prepare Homemade Pasta as directed above, *except* add herb to flour mixture.
Spinach Pasta **3 tablespoons water** **⅓ cup very finely chopped cooked spinach, well drained**	Prepare Homemade Pasta as directed above, *except* use the 3 tablespoons water and add the spinach to the egg mixture.

Nutrition information per ounce: 70 calories, 2 g protein, 12 g carbohydrate, 1 g fat (0 g saturated), 27 mg cholesterol, 78 mg sodium, 34 mg potassium.

Chunky Vegetable Sauce

Tingle your taste buds with the fresh flavors in this vegetable combination. (Pictured on pages 50 and 94.)

1 cup chopped onion
½ cup coarsely chopped green pepper
¼ cup coarsely chopped carrot
¼ cup sliced celery
2 cloves garlic, minced
2 tablespoons olive oil, margarine,
  ***or* butter**

● In a large skillet cook onion, green pepper, carrot, celery, and garlic in hot olive oil, margarine, or butter till vegetables are tender.

3 large ripe fresh tomatoes, peeled and
  chopped (2 cups), *or* one 16-ounce
  can tomatoes, cut up
½ of a 6-ounce can (⅓ cup) tomato
  paste
¼ cup water
¾ teaspoon dried basil, crushed
½ teaspoon sugar
½ teaspoon salt
½ teaspoon dried oregano, crushed
¼ teaspoon dried thyme, crushed

● Carefully stir in the fresh or *undrained* tomatoes, tomato paste, water, basil, sugar, salt, oregano, thyme, and ⅛ teaspoon *pepper*. Bring to boiling; reduce heat. Cover and simmer for 30 minutes. If necessary, uncover and simmer for 10 to 15 minutes more or to desired consistency, stirring occasionally.

4 ounces packaged spaghetti, linguine,
  ***or* other pasta**

● Meanwhile, cook pasta (see chart, page 8). Immediately drain. Serve sauce over pasta. Makes 4 side-dish servings.

Nutrition information per serving: 228 calories, 6 g protein, 36 g carbohydrate, 8 g fat (1 g saturated), 0 mg cholesterol, 304 mg sodium, 533 mg potassium.

Shaping and Storing Pasta

You can make and shape pasta, then store it so it's ready when you are. Try these shapes and storing methods.

To shape pasta: After kneading and rolling homemade pasta dough (*see* recipe, page 9), cut it into one of the following shapes.

● *Lasagna:* Cut into strips about 2½ inches wide. Then cut into desired lengths.

● *Farfalle:* Cut into 2x1-inch rectangles. Pinch centers to form bow ties.

● *Tripolini:* Cut into 1-inch circles. Pinch centers, forming butterfly shapes.

● *Linguine or fettuccine:* After rolling dough and letting it stand, loosely roll up dough jelly-roll style; cut into ⅛-inch-wide slices for linguine or ¼-inch-wide slices for fettuccine. Shake strands to separate. Cut into 12-inch lengths, if needed.

To store pasta: After shaping pasta, hang it from a pasta drying rack or clothes hanger, or spread it on a wire rack. Let dry overnight or till completely dry. Place in an airtight container and refrigerate up to 3 days. *Or,* dry the pasta at least 1 hour. Seal it in a freezer bag or container. Freeze for up to 8 months.

Fettuccine alla Carbonara

6 slices bacon, cut up **6 ounces packaged fettuccine, linguine,** ***or* other pasta**	● In a large skillet cook bacon till crisp. Drain bacon on paper towels. Cook pasta (*see* chart, page 8). Immediately drain. Return pasta to the warm saucepan.
1 beaten egg **1 cup light cream *or* milk** **2 tablespoons margarine *or* butter**	● Meanwhile, in a small saucepan combine the egg, light cream, and margarine. Cook and stir over medium heat. Continue cooking egg mixture till it just coats a metal spoon (about 6 minutes). Immediately pour egg mixture over the pasta and toss till well coated.
½ cup grated Parmesan cheese **¼ cup snipped parsley** **Coarsely ground black pepper**	● Add the Parmesan cheese, parsley, and bacon. Toss gently till well mixed. Transfer to a warm serving dish. Sprinkle with pepper. Serve immediately. Makes 6 side-dish servings.

Nutrition information per serving: 272 calories, 11 g protein, 24 g carbohydrate, 15 g fat (6 g saturated), 61 mg cholesterol, 301 mg sodium, 106 mg potassium.

Creamy Tomato Sauce

Boost this side dish to a main dish for four people by adding ¾ pound bulk Italian sausage, cooked and drained.

¾ cup chopped onion **2 cloves garlic, minced** **2 tablespoons margarine *or* butter**	● In a medium saucepan cook onion and garlic in hot margarine or butter till onion is tender but not brown.

2 14½-ounce cans whole Italian-style
    tomatoes, cut up, *or* 2 pounds ripe
    fresh plum tomatoes, peeled and
    chopped
½ teaspoon sugar
¼ teaspoon salt
⅛ teaspoon pepper
	● Carefully stir in the *undrained* or fresh tomatoes, sugar, salt, and pepper. Bring to boiling; reduce heat. Simmer, uncovered, about 30 minutes or to desired consistency, stirring occasionally.

½ cup whipping cream *or* light cream **2 tablespoons snipped parsley**	● Slowly add the cream, stirring constantly. Cook and stir for 3 minutes more. Remove from heat. Stir in parsley.
8 ounces packaged spaghetti, capellini, ***or* other pasta**	● Meanwhile, cook pasta (*see* chart, page 8). Immediately drain. Serve sauce over pasta. Makes 8 side-dish servings.

Nutrition information per serving: 210 calories, 5 g protein, 28 g carbohydrate, 9 g fat (4 g saturated), 20 mg cholesterol, 275 mg sodium, 271 mg potassium.

Pasta Fix-Ups

In a hurry and need a quick side dish? Choose your favorite pasta and one of these ideas, and you're set—pasta favorites in minutes!

Idea 1: Cook 4 ounces packaged *pasta* (see chart, page 8). Drain. In same warm pan cook ½ teaspoon *bottled minced garlic* in 1 tablespoon hot *olive oil* for 15 seconds. Add ¼ cup snipped, drained *sun-dried tomatoes* (oil pack), 1 tablespoon drained *capers*, and the cooked pasta. Toss till mixed. Makes 4 side-dish servings.
Nutrition information per serving: 180 calories, 5 g protein, 28 g carbohydrate, 6 g fat (1 g saturated), 0 mg cholesterol, 39 mg sodium, 265 mg potassium.

Idea 2: Cook packaged *pasta* (see chart, page 8). Drain. In same warm pan toss *margarine or butter*, grated *Parmesan cheese or Romano cheese,* and the cooked pasta. Add a few sliced pitted *ripe olives* or sliced *pimiento-stuffed olives*. Toss till mixed.

Idea 3: Cook 4 ounces packaged *pasta* (see chart, page 8). Drain. In same warm pan combine 2 cups hot cooked *vegetables*, ⅓ cup *light cream or milk*, ⅓ cup grated *Parmesan cheese*, 2 tablespoons *margarine or butter*, and the cooked pasta. Toss gently till well coated. Makes 4 side-dish servings.
Nutrition information per serving: 266 calories, 10 g protein, 35 g carbohydrate, 11 g fat (4 g saturated), 13 mg cholesterol, 233 mg sodium, 190 mg potassium.

Idea 4: Cook 4 ounces packaged *pasta* (see chart, page 8). Drain. In same warm pan toss ½ cup shredded *mozzarella or provolone cheese*; ⅓ cup snipped *salami, fully cooked ham, mortadella, or pepperoni;* ⅓ cup *whipping cream*; and the cooked pasta. Cook and stir over medium heat for 3 to 4 minutes or till cheese melts and sauce thickens slightly. Makes 4 side-dish servings.
Nutrition information per serving: 269 calories, 11 g protein, 23 g carbohydrate, 15 g fat (8 g saturated), 46 mg cholesterol, 339 mg sodium, 81 mg potassium.

Idea 5: Cook 4 ounces packaged *pasta* (see chart, page 8). Drain. In same warm pan cook ⅓ cup chopped *onion* and 1 tablespoon dried *parsley flakes* in 1 tablespoon *margarine or butter* till onion is tender. Stir in ¼ teaspoon *garlic powder*. Add pasta and toss till mixed. Makes 4 side-dish servings.

Nutrition information per serving: 136 calories, 4 g protein, 23 g carbohydrate, 3 g fat (1 g saturated), 0 mg cholesterol, 36 mg sodium, 29 mg potassium.

Idea 7: Cook 4 ounces packaged *pasta* (see chart, page 8). Drain. In same warm pan heat half of an 8-ounce container *soft-style cream cheese with chives and onion*, ¼ cup *milk*, and 1 tablespoon dried *parsley flakes* over medium-low heat till cheese melts and mixture is warm, stirring occasionally. Stir in ¼ cup grated *Parmesan or Romano cheese*. Add pasta and toss till well mixed. Makes 4 side-dish servings.

Nutrition information per serving: 186 calories, 7 g protein, 24 g carbohydrate, 7 g fat (4 g saturated), 5 mg cholesterol, 184 sodium, 34 potassium.

Idea 6: Cook packaged *pasta* (see chart, page 8). Drain. In same warm pan toss cooked pasta with hot *spaghetti sauce*. Divide pasta mixture among individual au gratin dishes or 6-ounce custard cups. Sprinkle shredded *mozzarella cheese* over each. Place dishes or cups in a baking pan. Bake in a 400° oven for 5 to 8 minutes or till bubbly.

Creamy White Clam Sauce

8 ounces packaged linguine, spaghetti, *or* **other pasta**	● Cook pasta (see chart, page 8). Immediately drain.
2 6½-ounce cans minced clams **Light cream** *or* **milk**	● Meanwhile, drain clams, reserving liquid. Add enough light cream or milk to the reserved liquid to make 1¾ cups.
½ cup chopped onion **2 cloves garlic, minced** **2 tablespoons margarine** *or* **butter** **¼ cup all-purpose flour** **½ teaspoon dried basil** *or* **oregano, crushed** **¼ teaspoon salt** **¼ teaspoon pepper** **¼ cup snipped parsley** **¼ cup dry white wine**	● For sauce, in a medium saucepan cook the onion and garlic in hot margarine or butter till onion is tender but not brown. Stir in the flour, basil or oregano, salt, and pepper. Add the cream mixture all at once. Cook and stir till thickened and bubbly. Cook and stir 1 minute more. Stir in the parsley, wine, and clams. Heat through.
¼ cup grated Parmesan cheese	● Serve sauce over pasta. Sprinkle with Parmesan cheese. Makes 4 main-dish servings.

Nutrition information per serving: 466 calories, 25 g protein, 56 g carbohydrate, 14 g fat (5 g saturated), 53 mg cholesterol, 467 mg sodium, 456 mg potassium.

Gorgonzola-Sauced Pasta

A sprinkling of nuts is all it takes to accent the full flavor of the cheese.

4 ounces packaged vermicelli, gemelli, *or* **other pasta**	● Cook pasta (see chart, page 8). Immediately drain. Return pasta to the warm saucepan.
1 tablespoon margarine *or* **butter** **½ cup crumbled Gorgonzola** *or* **blue cheese (2 ounces)** **¼ cup light cream** *or* **milk** **1 tablespoon snipped fresh basil** *or* **1 teaspoon dried basil, crushed** **Dash white pepper**	● Meanwhile, in a small saucepan melt margarine or butter. Add the Gorgonzola or blue cheese, light cream or milk, basil, and white pepper. Cook and stir over medium heat just till mixture is smooth and heated through.
¼ cup grated Parmesan cheese **2 tablespoons toasted pine nuts** *or* **toasted, chopped pecans** *or* **walnuts**	● Stir in Parmesan cheese. Pour sauce over pasta. Gently toss till pasta is coated. Transfer to a warm serving dish. Sprinkle with nuts. Serve immediately. Makes 4 side-dish servings.

Nutrition information per serving: 256 calories, 11 g protein, 24 g carbohydrate, 14 g fat (6 g saturated), 22 mg cholesterol, 392 mg sodium, 106 mg potassium.

Hot 'n' Spicy Sauce

For a fiery hot version, try using "hot" Italian sausage.

¾ **pound bulk Italian sausage**
½ **cup chopped onion**
¼ **cup finely chopped green pepper**
2 **cloves garlic, minced**

● In a large saucepan cook the Italian sausage, onion, green pepper, and garlic till sausage is brown. Drain fat.

1 **28-ounce can tomatoes, cut up**
1 **6-ounce can tomato paste**
½ **teaspoon salt**
½ **teaspoon dried oregano, crushed**
½ **teaspoon dried basil, crushed**
¼ **teaspoon pepper**
¼ **teaspoon ground red pepper**

● Carefully stir in the *undrained* tomatoes, tomato paste, salt, oregano, basil, pepper, and red pepper. Bring to boiling; reduce heat. Cover and simmer for 30 minutes. Then uncover and simmer for 10 to 15 minutes more or to desired consistency, stirring occasionally.

8 **ounces packaged spaghetti, fusilli,**
   ***or* other pasta**

● Meanwhile, cook pasta (see chart, page 8). Immediately drain. Serve sauce over pasta. Makes 4 main-dish servings.

Nutrition information per serving: 480 calories, 23 g protein, 63 g carbohydrate, 16 g fat (5 g saturated), 44 mg cholesterol, 1,144 mg sodium, 1,068 mg potassium.

Fettuccine Alfredo

Indulge in this rich and creamy dish that's a favorite of Italian cooks.

½ **cup light cream *or* whipping cream**
3 **tablespoons margarine *or* butter**

● Let light cream or whipping cream, and margarine or butter come to room temperature (allow about 40 minutes).

8 **ounces packaged fettuccine, linguine,**
   ***or* other pasta**

● Meanwhile, cook pasta (see chart, page 8). Immediately drain. Return pasta to the warm saucepan.

½ **cup grated Parmesan cheese**
   Coarsely ground black pepper

● Add the Parmesan cheese, light cream or whipping cream, and margarine or butter to the pasta. Toss gently till pasta is well coated. Transfer to a warm serving dish. Sprinkle with pepper. Serve immediately. Makes 6 side-dish servings.

Nutrition information per serving: 248 calories, 8 g protein, 30 g carbohydrate, 11 g fat (4 g saturated), 13 mg cholesterol, 203 mg sodium, 37 mg potassium.

Classic Spaghetti Sauce

¾ **pound ground beef *or* bulk pork sausage**
1 **cup chopped onion**
½ **cup chopped green pepper**
¼ **cup chopped celery**
2 **cloves garlic, minced**

● In a large saucepan or Dutch oven, cook ground beef or pork sausage, onion, green pepper, celery, and garlic till meat is brown. Drain fat.

2 **16-ounce cans tomatoes, cut up**
1 **6-ounce can tomato paste**
⅓ **cup water**
2 **tablespoons snipped parsley**
1 **teaspoon sugar**
1 **teaspoon dried basil, crushed**
1 **teaspoon dried oregano, crushed**
½ **teaspoon salt**
½ **teaspoon dried marjoram, crushed**
¼ **teaspoon pepper**

● Carefully stir in the *undrained* tomatoes, tomato paste, water, parsley, sugar, basil, oregano, salt, marjoram, and pepper. Bring to boiling; reduce heat. Cover and simmer for 30 minutes. Uncover and simmer for 10 to 15 minutes more or to desired consistency, stirring occasionally.

8 **ounces packaged spaghetti, vermicelli, *or* other pasta**
Grated Parmesan cheese (optional)

● Meanwhile, cook pasta (see chart, page 8). Immediately drain. Serve sauce over pasta. If desired, sprinkle with Parmesan cheese. Makes 4 or 5 main-dish servings.

Nutrition information per serving: 490 calories, 28 g protein, 67 g carbohydrate, 14 g fat (5 g saturated), 56 mg cholesterol, 724 mg sodium, 1,231 mg potassium.

Pesto

To store extra Pesto, divide into recipe-size portions, and place in airtight containers. Chill for up to 2 days or freeze up to 1 month. Before serving, bring to room temperature.

1 **cup firmly packed fresh basil leaves**
½ **cup firmly packed parsley sprigs with stems removed**
½ **cup grated Parmesan *or* Romano cheese**
¼ **cup olive oil *or* cooking oil**
¼ **cup pine nuts, walnuts, *or* almonds**
1 **large clove garlic, sliced**

● For pesto, in a blender container or food processor bowl combine basil; parsley; Parmesan or Romano cheese; olive oil or cooking oil; pine nuts, walnuts, or almonds; garlic; and ¼ teaspoon *salt*. Cover, and blend or process with several on-off turns till a paste forms, stopping the machine several times and scraping the sides.

4 **ounces packaged fusilli, spaghetti, *or* other pasta**

● To serve pesto with pasta, cook pasta (see chart, page 8). Immediately drain. Add a *third* of the pesto (about ¼ cup) to pasta, and toss. Makes 4 side-dish servings.

Nutrition information per serving: 288 calories, 9 g protein, 24 g carbohydrate, 18 g fat (4 g saturated), 8 mg cholesterol, 333 mg sodium, 145 mg potassium.

Spaghetti and Meatballs

1 cup sliced fresh mushrooms
¾ cup chopped onion
2 cloves garlic, minced
2 tablespoons olive oil *or* cooking oil

● In a Dutch oven cook mushrooms, onion, and garlic in hot olive oil or cooking oil till onion is tender but not brown.

2 16-ounce cans tomatoes, cut up
1 6-ounce can tomato paste
2 tablespoons snipped parsley
2 teaspoons dried Italian seasoning, crushed
1 teaspoon sugar
¾ teaspoon salt
¼ teaspoon pepper

● Carefully stir in the *undrained* tomatoes, tomato paste, parsley, Italian seasoning, sugar, salt, and pepper. Bring to boiling; reduce heat. Cover and simmer for 30 minutes.

1 beaten egg
¾ cup soft bread crumbs (1 slice)
¼ cup finely chopped onion
2 tablespoons finely chopped green pepper
¼ teaspoon salt
¼ teaspoon dried oregano, crushed
1 pound ground beef *or* bulk pork sausage
1 tablespoon cooking oil

● Meanwhile, in a large mixing bowl combine egg, bread crumbs, onion, green pepper, salt, and oregano. Add ground beef or sausage; mix well. Shape into 30 meatballs. In a large skillet cook meatballs, half at a time, in the cooking oil for 8 to 10 minutes or till no pink remains. Drain well. Add meatballs to the sauce. Cook, uncovered, for 10 to 15 minutes or to desired consistency, stirring occasionally.

8 ounces packaged spaghetti, linguine, *or* other pasta

● Cook pasta (see chart, page 8). Immediately drain. Serve sauce and meatballs over pasta. Makes 4 to 6 main-dish servings.

Nutrition information per serving: 680 calories, 36 g protein, 71 g carbohydrate, 30 g fat (8 g saturated), 127 mg cholesterol, 1,060 mg sodium, 1,329 mg potassium.

To make meatballs of equal size, shape meat mixture into a 6x5-inch rectangle. Using a long knife, cut into thirty 1-inch squares. Then roll each square into a ball.

Primavera Pasta Pie

4 ounces packaged spaghetti
1 beaten egg
⅓ cup grated Parmesan cheese
1 tablespoon margarine *or* butter

● For pasta crust, cook spaghetti (see chart, page 8). Immediately drain. In a medium mixing bowl stir together the egg, Parmesan cheese, and margarine or butter. Stir in the hot spaghetti. Grease a 9-inch pie plate. Press the spaghetti mixture evenly into bottom and up sides of the prepared pie plate. Set aside.

2 cups broccoli flowerets
1 small sweet red *or* green pepper, cut into strips
1 medium onion, sliced and separated into rings
2 tablespoons margarine *or* butter
2 cups chopped cooked chicken *or* turkey
¼ cup grated Parmesan cheese
¾ teaspoon dried Italian seasoning, crushed
¼ teaspoon salt

● In a large skillet cook the broccoli, red or green pepper, and onion in hot margarine or butter till vegetables are *just* crisp-tender. Stir in chicken or turkey, Parmesan cheese, Italian seasoning, and salt. Remove from heat. Spoon vegetable mixture into pasta crust.

2 beaten eggs
½ cup whipping cream *or* light cream
2 tablespoons grated Parmesan cheese

● In a small mixing bowl stir together the eggs and whipping cream. Pour over vegetable mixture in the pasta crust. Bake, covered, in a 350° oven for 25 minutes; uncover and sprinkle with Parmesan cheese. Bake for 10 minutes more. Let stand 10 minutes. Cut into wedges. Makes 6 main-dish servings.

Nutrition information per serving: 374 calories, 26 g protein, 20 g carbohydrate, 21 g fat (9 g saturated), 180 mg cholesterol, 415 mg sodium, 270 mg potassium.

Hot Pasta Tips

These hints will help you keep pasta just the way you like it—piping hot.
● Use a warm serving dish. To warm your serving dish, fill it with hot water, then let it stand a few minutes to absorb the heat. Drain the pasta in a colander. Next, empty the dish, and wipe it dry. Add the pasta, and serve immediately.

● Drain pasta quickly. Give the colander a few quick shakes to speed up the process.
● If you can't serve the pasta right away, return the pasta to the pan it was cooked in. Or, for a delay of 10 minutes or more, leave the pasta in, or transfer it to, a *metal* colander, then place colander over a pan containing a small amount of boiling water. Keep the water boiling. Coat pasta with a little margarine to prevent sticking. Cover the colander. Serve the pasta as soon as possible.

Primavera Pasta Pie

Sausage and Mushroom Pasta Pie

A touch of American ingenuity—spaghetti, sauce, and cheese baked as a pie!

4 ounces packaged spaghetti
1 beaten egg
⅓ cup grated Parmesan *or* Romano cheese
1 tablespoon margarine *or* butter

● For pasta crust, cook spaghetti (see chart, page 8). Immediately drain. In a medium mixing bowl combine egg, cheese, and margarine. Stir in hot spaghetti. Grease a 9-inch pie plate. Press the spaghetti mixture evenly into bottom and up sides of the prepared pie plate. Set aside.

1 beaten egg
1 cup cream-style cottage cheese
1 tablespoon snipped parsley
1 4-ounce can sliced mushrooms, drained

● In a small mixing bowl stir together egg, cottage cheese, and parsley. Spread cottage cheese mixture evenly over the pasta crust. Sprinkle with mushrooms. Set aside.

¾ pound bulk Italian sausage *or* bulk pork sausage
½ cup chopped onion
¼ cup chopped green pepper
1 cup purchased meatless spaghetti sauce
¼ teaspoon garlic powder
1 tablespoon grated Parmesan *or* Romano cheese
½ cup shredded mozzarella cheese (2 ounces)

● In a large skillet cook sausage, onion, and green pepper till meat is brown. Drain fat. Then stir in the spaghetti sauce and garlic powder; heat through. Spoon meat mixture over cottage cheese mixture and mushrooms. Sprinkle with Parmesan or Romano cheese. Bake in a 350° oven about 25 minutes or till crust is set. Sprinkle with mozzarella cheese. Let stand 5 minutes. Cut into wedges. Makes 5 main-dish servings.

Nutrition information per serving: 467 calories, 28 g protein, 31 g carbohydrate, 26 g fat (10 g saturated), 142 mg cholesterol, 1,210 mg sodium, 468 mg potassium.

Measuring Dry Pasta

If you want to end up with the proper amount of pasta, but you don't have a kitchen scale, try these guidelines.
● Four ounces of uncooked small pasta, such as conchiglie or cavatelli, measures about 1 cup.
● Four ounces of uncooked medium pasta, such as rigatoni or mostaccioli, measures about 3 cups.
● Four ounces of uncooked long pasta with a small diameter, such as vermicelli or spaghetti, measures about 1 inch in diameter when held together in a bunch.

Lasagna

In Italy, wide lasagna noodles are frequently used in this main dish as well as in a variety of other dishes.

½ **pound bulk pork sausage, bulk Italian sausage, *or* ground beef**
2 **cups sliced fresh mushrooms**
¾ **cup chopped onion**
½ **cup chopped green pepper**
2 **cloves garlic, minced**

● For meat sauce, in a large saucepan cook pork sausage, Italian sausage, or ground beef, mushrooms, onion, green pepper, and garlic till the meat is brown and vegetables are tender. Drain fat.

1 **8-ounce can tomato sauce**
1 **7½-ounce can tomatoes, cut up**
1 **6-ounce can tomato paste**
1½ **teaspoons dried basil, crushed**
1 **teaspoon dried oregano, crushed**
½ **teaspoon fennel seed, crushed (optional)**

● Carefully stir in the tomato sauce, the *undrained* tomatoes, tomato paste, basil, oregano, and, if desired, fennel. Bring to boiling; reduce heat. Cover and simmer for 15 minutes, stirring occasionally.

6 **packaged lasagna noodles**

● Meanwhile, cook lasagna noodles (see chart, page 8). Immediately drain.

1 **beaten egg**
1½ **cups ricotta cheese *or* cream-style cottage cheese, drained**
¼ **cup grated Parmesan *or* Romano cheese**
¼ **teaspoon pepper**

● For filling, in a small mixing bowl stir together the egg, ricotta cheese or cottage cheese, Parmesan or Romano cheese, and pepper.

1½ **cups shredded mozzarella *or* provolone cheese (6 ounces)**
¼ **cup grated Parmesan *or* Romano cheese**

● Layer *half* of the cooked noodles in a 12x7½x2-inch baking dish. Spread with *half* of the filling. Top with *half* of the meat sauce and *half* of the mozzarella or provolone cheese. Repeat layers. Sprinkle Parmesan or Romano cheese over top. Bake in a 375° oven for 30 to 35 minutes or till heated through. Let stand 10 minutes. Makes 6 to 8 main-dish servings.

Nutrition information per serving: 439 calories, 27 g protein, 34 g carbohydrate, 22 g fat (12 g saturated), 103 mg cholesterol, 871 mg sodium, 846 mg potassium.

Cheesy Manicotti

In a hurry? Just substitute purchased spaghetti sauce with meat for the homemade sauce. (Pictured on the cover.)

8 packaged manicotti shells *or* 16 packaged conchiglioni (jumbo shells)

● Cook manicotti or conchiglioni (see chart, page 8). Immediately drain. Rinse with cold water, then drain well.

2 beaten eggs
2 cups shredded mozzarella cheese (8 ounces)
1½ cups ricotta cheese
⅓ cup grated Parmesan cheese
1 tablespoon snipped parsley
¼ teaspoon pepper

● Meanwhile, for filling, in a medium mixing bowl stir together the eggs, mozzarella cheese, ricotta cheese, Parmesan cheese, parsley, and pepper.

2 cups Classic Spaghetti Sauce (see recipe, page 16) *or* Hot 'n' Spicy Sauce (see recipe, page 15)
¼ cup grated Parmesan *or* Romano cheese

● *To fill manicotti shells*, stuff about ⅓ cup of the filling into *each* cooked shell. *To fill conchiglioni*, stuff about *3 tablespoons* of the filling into *each* cooked shell. Arrange filled manicotti or conchiglioni in a 12x7½x2-inch baking dish. Pour sauce over the top. Sprinkle with Parmesan or Romano cheese. Bake, covered, in a 350° oven 35 to 40 minutes or till heated through. Makes 4 main-dish servings.

Nutrition information per serving: 596 calories, 44 g protein, 32 g carbohydrate, 33 g fat (18 g saturated), 216 mg cholesterol, 880 mg sodium, 656 mg potassium.

To successfully fill manicotti shells, use a spoon with a smaller diameter than the shell, and stuff about ⅓ *cup* of the filling into *each* cooked shell. Using a small spoon will help you reach the center without tearing the pasta.

Chicken Lasagna Rolls

In Italy, creamy white sauce is an integral part of many types of lasagna dishes.

8 packaged no-boil lasagna noodles *or* regular lasagna noodles

● Soak no-boil lasagna noodles in warm water for 10 minutes. Drain. *Or,* cook regular lasagna noodles (*see chart, page 8*). Immediately drain. Rinse with *cold* water; drain again.

1 10-ounce package frozen chopped spinach

● Cook frozen spinach according to package directions. Drain well, pressing out excess liquid.

1½ cups shredded Bel Paese *or* fontina cheese (6 ounces)
1½ cups chopped cooked chicken
1 cup ricotta cheese
¼ cup grated Parmesan cheese
¼ teaspoon pepper

● In a medium mixing bowl stir together the Bel Paese or fontina cheese, chicken, ricotta cheese, Parmesan cheese, pepper, and the cooked spinach.

● To assemble rolls, spread about *½ cup* cheese mixture on *each* noodle. Roll up jelly-roll style beginning from one of the short sides. Place seam side down in a lightly greased 12x7½x2-inch baking dish. Set aside.

½ cup chopped onion
2 cloves garlic, minced
2 tablespoons margarine *or* butter
2 tablespoons all-purpose flour
Dash pepper
1½ cups milk
¼ cup grated Parmesan cheese

● For sauce, in a medium saucepan cook onion and garlic in hot margarine or butter till onion is tender but not brown. Stir in flour and pepper. Add milk all at once. Cook and stir till thickened and bubbly. Cook and stir 1 minute more. Stir in *2 tablespoons* of the Parmesan cheese. Pour sauce over rolls. Sprinkle with remaining Parmesan cheese. Cover and bake in a 375° oven for 30 to 35 minutes or till filling is heated through. Makes 4 main-dish servings.

Nutrition information per serving: 716 calories, 50 g protein, 49 g carbohydrate, 35 g fat (18 g saturated), 141 mg cholesterol, 457 mg sodium, 728 mg potassium.

Choosing a Pasta

Beyond the basic spaghetti and fettuccine, there is a vast selection of pasta in many shapes, sizes, and flavors. Basic pasta can be found in local supermarkets, but those that are more uncommon, such as tomato-flavored fettuccine, will need to be purchased in food specialty stores.

To help you select the kind you want, take a look at the varieties below. We tried to show a sampling of what's available in different sizes, shapes, and flavors, as well as in dry, packaged or fresh, refrigerated forms. We've listed the common Italian name along with a short description. If the name differs from what you find in your supermarket, look for the same pasta by shape, or choose a substitute.

Mafalda
(flat ribbons about ¾ inch wide)

Fusilli
(twisted spaghetti)

Ziti
(long tubular pasta)

Conchigliette
(small shells)

Conchiglie
(medium or large shells)

Tortellini
(little stuffed rings)

Tripolini
(tiny bows or wing nuts)

Farfalle
(butterflies or bow ties)

Ravioli
(stuffed pasta squares)

Rotelle
(corkscrew or spiral macaroni)

Gemelli
(twin twists of spaghetti)

Lasagna Noodles
(flat ribbons about 2 inches wide)

Fettuccine
(flat ribbons about ¼ inch wide)

Linguine
(flat ribbons about ⅛ inch wide)

Conchiglioni
(jumbo shells)

Rigatoni
(ridged pasta tubes)

Manicotti
(large, diagonally cut tubes)

Spaghetti
(round, thin strands)

Mostaccioli or Penne
(smooth pasta tubes resembling quill pens)

Ruote
(wagon wheels)

Cavatelli
(curled shells with ridges)

Vermicelli
(thin spaghetti)

Spaghettini
(very thin spaghetti)

Orzo or Rosamarina
(barley-shaped, ricelike pasta)

Acini di pepe
(little peppercorns)

Anelli
(little rings)

Capellini
(fine angel hairs)

Spinach and Pasta Pinwheels

You can make the pasta rolls up to a day ahead, then slice and bake them in time for dinner.

⅓ recipe Homemade Pasta dough
(see recipe, page 9)

● Divide pasta dough in half. On a lightly floured surface roll each half into a 12x6-inch rectangle. Let stand for 20 minutes. Then in a 4½-quart kettle or Dutch oven, bring salted water to boiling. Immerse 1 pasta sheet into the water. Return to boiling. Cook pasta about 3 minutes or till al dente (tender but slightly firm). Use a slotted spoon to carefully lift pasta and transfer it to a colander. Rinse with cold water. Drain well. Carefully spread on a cloth towel. Let stand, uncovered, for 15 to 20 minutes to dry. Repeat with remaining pasta sheet.

1 10-ounce package frozen chopped spinach
1 beaten egg
1¼ cups ricotta cheese
½ of an 8-ounce package cream cheese, softened
½ cup finely shredded Parmesan cheese
2 tablespoons finely chopped onion
⅛ teaspoon pepper

● Meanwhile, for filling, cook spinach according to package directions. Drain well, pressing out excess liquid. In a medium mixing bowl stir together the egg, ricotta cheese, cream cheese, Parmesan cheese, onion, and pepper. Add the spinach and mix well.

1 6-ounce package sliced fully cooked ham

● To assemble, arrange the ham over the pasta sheets. Spread with the filling to within ¼ inch of the edges. Roll up jelly-roll style, starting from one of the short sides. Cover tightly and chill for 1 to 24 hours. Trim uneven edges of rolls. Cut each roll into 6 even slices. Place the slices, cut side down, in a 12x7½x2-inch baking dish. Bake, covered, in a 375° oven about 35 minutes or till heated through.

3 tablespoons margarine *or* butter
2 tablespoons all-purpose flour
¼ teaspoon salt
Dash pepper
Dash ground nutmeg
1½ cups milk

● Meanwhile, for sauce, in a medium saucepan melt margarine or butter. Stir in the flour, salt, pepper, and nutmeg. Add milk all at once. Cook and stir till thickened and bubbly. Cook and stir for 1 minute more.

● To serve, divide sauce among individual plates. Place pasta pinwheels atop sauce. Makes 4 to 6 main-dish servings.

Nutrition information per serving: 615 calories, 36 g protein, 31 g carbohydrate, 39 g fat (19 g saturated), 198 mg cholesterol, 1,366 mg sodium, 650 mg potassium.

Try these helpful hints when making the Spinach and Pasta Pinwheels.

To cook the large pasta sheets, use both hands to lift a pasta sheet, then carefully immerse the sheet into the boiling water. Handle the sheets gently to avoid tearing.

To roll up the pasta and filling, start from one of the short sides and tightly roll up the pasta jelly-roll style, using a towel as necessary to lift pasta and aid in rolling.

To trim the uneven edges from the rolls, use a very sharp knife. Then cut each pasta roll into 6 even slices.

MEATS & POULTRY

When it comes to preparing meats and poultry, Italian cooks have
devised many delectable ways. Here is a collection of
recipes including simple dishes, such as Italian-Style Pepper Steak
and Turkey Piccata, as well as fancier fare,
such as Seasoned Roast Lamb and Cheese-Stuffed Chicken Breasts.

Italian Beef Roll

1 **pound beef top round steak, cut
½ inch thick**
3 **ounces thinly sliced cappicola *or*
fully cooked ham**
1 **beaten egg**
½ **pound lean ground beef**
½ **cup fresh *or* frozen peas**
¼ **cup grated Parmesan cheese**
¼ **cup snipped parsley**

● With a meat mallet, pound steak into a 12x8-inch rectangle, working from center to edges. Arrange cappicola or ham on steak, overlapping as necessary. Combine the egg, ground beef, peas, Parmesan cheese, and parsley; spread over meat. Roll up jelly-roll style, beginning from one of the short sides. Tie meat in 3 or 4 places with string.

1 **tablespoon cooking oil**
1 **large onion, chopped (1 cup)**
1 **clove garlic, minced**
1 **cup beef broth**
½ **cup dry red wine *or* beef broth**
¼ **cup tomato paste**

● In a large skillet brown meat on all sides in hot oil. Add onion and garlic, and cook till onion is tender. Stir in beef broth, wine, and tomato paste. Heat to boiling. Reduce heat. Cover and simmer about 45 minutes or till meat is tender. Remove meat. If necessary, boil broth mixture rapidly, uncovered, for 1 to 2 minutes or till reduced to 2 cups. Skim off fat.

6 **ounces packaged linguine, fettuccine,
or other pasta, cooked and drained
(see chart, page 8)**

● Remove strings and slice meat into 6 or 12 slices. Arrange meat slices on pasta. Spoon broth mixture over top. Makes 6 servings.

Nutrition information per serving: 408 calories, 35 g protein, 29 g carbohydrate, 15 g fat (5 g saturated), 117 mg cholesterol, 462 mg sodium, 591 mg potassium.

Grilled Italian Beef Roll
1 **1-pound beef flank steak**

Prepare Italian Beef Roll as above, *except* omit beef top round steak and cooking oil. Score beef flank steak on one side by making shallow cuts at 1-inch intervals diagonally across steak in a diamond pattern. With a meat mallet, pound steak into a 12x8-inch rectangle, working from center to edges. Stuff and roll as above. Skewer with wooden toothpicks at about 1-inch intervals. Cut roll between toothpicks into 6 slices (about 1½ inches thick). Grill directly over medium-hot coals for 8 minutes. Turn and grill to desired doneness, allowing 8 to 10 minutes more for medium.

In a saucepan combine the onion, garlic, beef broth, wine, and tomato paste. Bring to boiling. Reduce heat and simmer, covered, about 20 minutes or till onion is tender. Uncover; boil gently about 5 minutes or till reduced to 2 cups. Serve as above.

Nutrition information per serving: 418 calories, 33 g protein, 29 g carbohydrate, 17 g fat (7 g saturated), 111 mg cholesterol, 472 mg sodium, 601 mg potassium.

Italian-Style Pepper Steak

Italian-Style Pepper Steak

2 medium green *and/or* sweet red
    peppers
½ cup chopped onion
2 cloves garlic, minced
1 tablespoon cooking oil

● Cut peppers into thin strips. In a large skillet cook peppers, onion, and garlic in hot cooking oil about 4 minutes or till crisp-tender. Remove vegetables from skillet. Keep warm.

¾ pound beef tenderloin, sliced **½** to **¾**
    inch thick, *or* **¾** pound beef top
    sirloin steak, cut **½** to **¾** inch thick
Salt

● Place meat in the same skillet. (Add more oil if necessary.) Sprinkle lightly with salt. Cook over medium-high heat about 4 minutes on each side or till slightly pink in center. Transfer to a serving platter. Keep warm.

¾ cup beef broth
½ teaspoon dried oregano *or* basil,
    crushed
2 medium tomatoes, seeded and
    chopped (1 cup)

● Cool skillet for 1 minute. Carefully add the beef broth and oregano or basil to skillet. Bring to boiling. Boil gently, uncovered, over medium heat for 2 to 3 minutes or till broth is reduced to ⅓ cup, scraping up browned bits in pan. Remove from heat. Stir in the cooked pepper mixture and tomatoes. Spoon onto platter with meat. Makes 4 servings.

Nutrition information per serving: 236 calories, 18 g protein, 7 g carbohydrate, 15 g fat (5 g saturated), 55 mg cholesterol, 225 mg sodium, 531 mg potassium.

Beef-Stuffed Peppers

4 medium green *or* sweet red peppers
    (6 ounces each)

● Cut tops from peppers. Remove seeds and membranes. Chop tops into pieces to make 2 tablespoons; set aside. Immerse peppers into *boiling* water 3 minutes or till crisp-tender. Drain; invert onto paper towels. Set aside.

¾ pound ground beef *or* ground pork
½ cup finely chopped onion
1 10-ounce package frozen chopped
    spinach, thawed and well drained
1½ cups Chunky Vegetable Sauce (see
    recipe, page 10) *or* purchased
    meatless chunky garden-style
    spaghetti sauce
1 beaten egg
¼ cup fine dry bread crumbs
¼ cup grated Parmesan *or* Romano
    cheese
1 teaspoon dried marjoram *or* basil,
    crushed
¼ teaspoon salt

● In a large skillet cook meat, onion, and the chopped pepper till meat is brown and onion is tender. Drain off excess fat. Stir in spinach, *¾ cup* of the sauce, the egg, bread crumbs, Parmesan cheese, marjoram, salt, and ⅛ teaspoon *pepper.* Mix well. Fill peppers with meat mixture, and place in an 8x8x2-inch baking dish. Bake, loosely covered with foil, in a 375° oven for 30 to 35 minutes or till heated through. Heat remaining sauce. Serve sauce with peppers. Makes 4 servings.

Nutrition information per serving: 370 calories, 25 g protein, 25 g carbohydrate, 20 g fat (7 g saturated), 113 mg cholesterol, 586 mg sodium, 990 mg potassium.

Cheesy Sausage Meat Loaf

Surprise! You'll find melted mozzarella hidden in the center.

1 beaten egg
¾ cup soft bread crumbs (1 slice)
¼ cup milk
¼ cup finely chopped onion
2 tablespoons finely chopped green pepper
1 teaspoon dried oregano, crushed
½ teaspoon garlic salt
1 pound ground beef
⅓ pound bulk Italian sausage

● In a large mixing bowl stir together the egg, bread crumbs, milk, onion, green pepper, oregano, and garlic salt. Add the ground beef and Italian sausage. Mix well.

4 ounces mozzarella cheese, cut into 3x1x½-inch sticks

● Place waxed paper in shallow baking pan. On waxed paper flatten meat mixture into a 10-inch square. Lay cheese sticks end to end near one edge to within ½ inch of the sides. Beginning with that edge and using waxed paper to lift meat, roll up jelly-roll style. Seal ends. Unroll onto pan, placing roll seam side down; discard waxed paper. Bake in a 350° oven 45 to 50 minutes or till juices run clear.

Note: To ensure that the meat mixture has reached the proper temperature of 170°, check the meat loaf once it is removed from the oven, using a meat or microwave thermometer.

1½ cups Creamy Tomato Sauce (see recipe, page 11) *or* Chunky Vegetable Sauce (see recipe, page 10)

● Let meat loaf stand for 5 minutes. Meanwhile, heat the sauce. Remove meat loaf from baking pan. Cut into slices. Serve sauce with meat loaf. Makes 6 servings.

Nutrition information per serving: 350 calories, 25 g protein, 9 g carbohydrate, 24 g fat (10 g saturated), 121 mg cholesterol, 662 mg sodium, 430 mg potassium.

To easily roll up the meat loaf, begin with the edge where the cheese is placed. Using the waxed paper to lift the meat, roll up jelly-roll style. Seal ends. Then roll meat loaf onto the pan, placing the seam side down.

Beef Braised in Barolo Wine

1 **2- to 2½-pound beef bottom round roast *or* beef chuck pot roast**
1 **cup Barolo wine *or* other dry red wine**
2 **cloves garlic, sliced**
2 **bay leaves**
2 **teaspoons juniper berries (optional)**
1 **teaspoon instant beef bouillon granules**
   Pinch dried thyme, crushed

● Trim fat from roast. Place roast in a plastic bag set in a shallow baking dish. For marinade, combine wine; garlic; bay leaves; juniper berries, if desired; beef bouillon granules; thyme; and 1 cup *water*. Pour over roast. Seal bag. Marinate in the refrigerator for 12 to 24 hours, turning the bag occasionally.

1 **tablespoon olive oil *or* cooking oil**
1 **medium onion, finely chopped**
1 **medium carrot, finely chopped**
1 **stalk celery, finely chopped**

● Remove roast, reserving marinade. Pat roast dry. In a 4-quart Dutch oven brown meat on all sides in hot oil. Drain off fat. Add onion, carrot, and celery. Strain marinade and add to Dutch oven. Heat to boiling. Reduce heat; cover and simmer about 2 hours or till meat is tender.

● Transfer meat to a serving platter. Boil cooking liquid, uncovered, for 5 to 10 minutes or till reduced to 1 cup. Pass with meat. Makes 6 servings.

Nutrition information per serving: 278 calories, 33 g protein, 3 g carbohydrate, 11 g fat (3 g saturated), 92 mg cholesterol, 241 mg sodium, 564 mg potassium.

Veal Parmigiana

1 **pound veal leg sirloin steak *or* veal leg round steak, cut ½ inch thick**

● Cut veal into 4 serving-size pieces. With a meat mallet, pound pieces to ⅛-inch thickness.

⅓ **cup fine dry Italian-seasoned bread crumbs**
3 **tablespoons grated Parmesan cheese**
½ **teaspoon dried oregano, crushed**
1 **beaten egg**
2 **tablespoons milk**
3 **tablespoons olive oil *or* cooking oil**

● In a shallow bowl stir together the bread crumbs, Parmesan cheese, and oregano. In another shallow bowl stir together the egg and milk. Dip veal pieces in egg mixture, then in crumb mixture to coat. In a 12-inch skillet, cook veal in hot oil for 2 to 3 minutes on each side or till golden. Remove skillet from heat.

1 **cup Creamy Tomato Sauce (see recipe, page 11) *or* Chunky Vegetable Sauce (see recipe, page 10)**
½ **cup shredded mozzarella cheese (2 ounces)**
1 **tablespoon grated Parmesan cheese**

● In a small saucepan heat the sauce to boiling. Spoon over veal in skillet. Top with mozzarella and Parmesan cheese. Cover; let stand 2 minutes or till cheese melts. Serves 4.

Nutrition information per serving: 388 calories, 29 g protein, 11 g carbohydrate, 25 g fat (8 g saturated), 183 mg cholesterol, 481 mg sodium, 444 mg potassium.

33

Veal Chops with Caper Sauce

An easy, yet elegant, dinner.

 4 **veal rib chops *or* veal loin chops, cut**
    ½ inch thick (1 to 1¼ pounds total)
 ¼ **cup all-purpose flour**
 1 **beaten egg**
 1 **tablespoon water**
 ⅓ **cup fine dry bread crumbs**
 2 **tablespoons olive oil *or* cooking oil**

● Trim excess fat from veal chops. Dip chops in flour, then in a mixture of the beaten egg and water, and then in bread crumbs. In a large skillet cook chops in hot olive oil or cooking oil over medium-low heat for 4 to 6 minutes on each side or till juices run clear. Transfer chops to a serving platter and keep warm.

 ⅓ **cup thinly sliced green onion**
 2 **tablespoons brandy**
 ⅔ **cup whipping cream**
 2 **tablespoons capers, drained**
 2 **tablespoons snipped parsley**

● In the same large skillet cook green onion over medium heat about 1 minute or till onion is tender. Remove from heat. Carefully stir in brandy, scraping up browned bits. Return to heat. Stir in whipping cream and capers. Bring to boiling. Boil for 2 to 3 minutes or till slightly thickened. Serve sauce over chops. Sprinkle with parsley. Makes 4 servings.

Nutrition information per serving: 374 calories, 15 g protein, 19 g carbohydrate, 26 g fat (12 g saturated), 166 mg cholesterol, 192 mg sodium, 229 mg potassium.

Italy's Finest Cured Meats

An array of cured meats is used by Italian cooks for everything from antipasto platters and late-night snacks to sandwiches and meat stuffings. Domestic versions are available at Italian specialty stores or deli counters.
● *Cappicola* is cured pork shoulder seasoned with ground hot or sweet peppers, paprika, salt, and sugar. Cappicola is typically used as a cold meat on antipasto platters and in sandwiches.
● *Mortadella*, a finely chopped pork that is studded with pork fat, is said to be the original bologna. Mortadella is most commonly used as a cold meat on antipasto platters and in sandwiches.
● *Prosciutto* is a dry-cured ham with a somewhat sweet flavor that is developed through a long curing process of at least 9 months. Prosciutto is served cold on antipasto platters and in sandwiches, or hot in meat fillings and pasta dishes.
● *Salami* is made from ground pork with some beef added. The difference from one salami to another depends on the type of grind, either fine or coarse, and the degree of flavor, which ranges from delicate, yet full-flavored, to garlicky and spicy. Salami is generally served cold for snacks, on antipasto platters, and in salads.

Spinach-Stuffed Veal Chops

½ cup chopped onion
½ cup finely chopped prosciutto *or* fully
   cooked ham
1 clove garlic, minced
1 tablespoon olive oil *or* cooking oil
1 10-ounce package frozen chopped
   spinach, thawed and well drained
½ cup shredded mozzarella cheese
   (2 ounces)
2 tablespoons grated Parmesan cheese
2 tablespoons toasted, chopped pine
   nuts *or* walnuts
1 teaspoon dried basil, crushed

● For stuffing, in a large skillet cook onion, prosciutto or ham, and garlic in hot olive oil or cooking oil till onion is tender but not brown. Add the spinach, mozzarella cheese, Parmesan cheese, pine nuts or walnuts, and basil. Stir till combined.

6 veal loin chops, cut 1 inch thick
   (2½ to 3 pounds total)

● Cut a pocket in each veal chop by cutting from the fat side almost to the bone. Spoon about ⅓ *cup* stuffing into *each* pocket. Secure with wooden toothpicks. Place chops on a rack in a roasting pan or shallow baking pan. Bake, uncovered, in a 350° oven for 45 to 60 minutes or till juices run clear. Remove toothpicks before serving. Makes 6 servings.

Nutrition information per serving: 206 calories, 25 g protein, 5 g carbohydrate, 10 g fat (3 g saturated), 99 mg cholesterol, 340 mg sodium, 435 mg potassium.

Veal with Tuna Sauce

Traditionally served chilled, this dish is equally good served warm.

1 pound veal leg round steak, cut ½
   inch thick

● Cut veal into 4 serving-size pieces. With a meat mallet, pound each piece to ¼-inch thickness. Set aside.

¼ cup finely chopped onion
1 clove garlic, minced
2 tablespoons cooking oil

● In a large skillet cook onion and garlic in hot cooking oil till onion is tender but not brown. Add veal pieces, and cook for 1 to 2 minutes on each side or till lightly browned. Remove veal from skillet; cover and chill.

½ recipe Tomatoey Tuna Sauce
   (see recipe, page 6), chilled

● Serve chilled Tomatoey Tuna Sauce over chilled veal. Makes 4 servings.

Nutrition information per serving: 327 calories, 35 g protein, 11 g carbohydrate, 16 g fat (3 g saturated), 137 mg cholesterol, 520 mg sodium, 841 mg potassium.

Prosciutto-Stuffed Pork Rolls

These tender pork rolls are nestled in a bed of pasta.

4 ounces prosciutto, chopped
½ cup shredded mozzarella *or* fontina cheese (2 ounces)
2 tablespoons snipped parsley
1 clove garlic, minced

● For filling, in a small mixing bowl stir together the prosciutto, mozzarella or fontina cheese, parsley, and garlic. Set aside.

4 4-ounce boneless pork loin chops, cut 1½ inches thick
1 tablespoon olive oil *or* cooking oil

● With a meat mallet, pound each pork chop to ⅛- to ¼-inch thickness. Place about *¼ cup* filling on *each* piece of meat. Roll up, jelly-roll style, folding in sides as you roll. Secure with wooden toothpicks or tie with string. In a large skillet brown meat rolls on all sides in hot olive oil or cooking oil. Drain off excess fat.

1 14½-ounce can whole Italian-style tomatoes, cut up, *or* one 14½-ounce can Italian-style stewed tomatoes
½ teaspoon dried basil, crushed
⅛ teaspoon pepper

● Carefully add the *undrained* tomatoes, basil, and pepper. Bring to boiling. Reduce heat and simmer, covered, about 30 minutes or till meat is tender. Remove toothpicks or string.

4 ounces packaged linguine, spaghetti, *or* other pasta, cooked and drained (see chart, page 8)
1 tablespoon water
2 teaspoons cornstarch

● Arrange hot cooked pasta on a platter. Add the meat rolls; keep warm. Stir together the water and cornstarch. Stir into tomato mixture. Cook and stir till thickened and bubbly; cook and stir for 2 minutes more. Serve over meat rolls and pasta. Makes 4 servings.

Nutrition information per serving: 449 calories, 43 g protein, 31 g carbohydrate, 17 g fat (5 g saturated), 107 mg cholesterol, 872 mg sodium, 779 mg potassium.

Prosciutto-Stuffed Beef Rolls
1 pound boneless beef top round steak, cut ½ inch thick
2 ounces prosciutto, chopped

Prepare Prosciutto-Stuffed Pork Rolls as directed above, *except* substitute the beef top round steak for the pork. Cut steak into 4 serving-size pieces. Pound and stuff with filling, using the 2 ounces prosciutto. Brown meat rolls and add sauce ingredients as directed, then simmer, covered, for 1 to 1¼ hours or till tender. Serve as above.

Nutrition information per serving: 392 calories, 36 g protein, 31 g carbohydrate, 13 g fat (4 g saturated), 85 mg cholesterol, 672 mg sodium, 706 mg potassium.

Prosciutto-Stuffed Pork Rolls

Pork Loin with Vegetable Sauce

Delicately seasoned with leeks and white wine.

**1 2- to 2½-pound pork loin roast,
    backbone loosened
3 medium leeks, sliced (1 cup)
½ cup finely chopped carrot
½ cup finely chopped celery
1 tablespoon cooking oil**

● Trim fat from pork roast. In a Dutch oven cook leeks, carrot, and celery in hot oil till vegetables are tender. Push vegetables to the side of the pan. Add roast to the pan. Brown well on all sides.

**½ cup dry white wine *or* water
½ teaspoon salt
¼ teaspoon pepper**

● Add white wine or water, salt, and pepper to the Dutch oven. Bring to boiling. Reduce heat. Cover and simmer about 1½ hours or till roast is tender and no pink remains.

● Transfer roast to a warm serving platter. Skim off any fat from pan juices. Pour pan juices and vegetables into a serving bowl. Pass with pork roast. Makes 6 servings.

Nutrition information per serving: 256 calories, 23 g protein, 4 g carbohydrate, 14 g fat (4 g saturated), 77 mg cholesterol, 259 mg sodium, 415 mg potassium.

Northern and Southern Food

Italian cuisine varies greatly between the northern and the southern regions. The northern regions tend to have foods that are creamy and mild. Ingredients such as butter, cream, and rice are often combined to make popular dishes such as Fettuccine Alfredo and Risotto.

In contrast, the foods in southern Italy are usually highly seasoned. Tomatoes, peppers, and olive oil are a few of the typical ingredients used to create hearty tomatoey sauces that are common in the south. The most familiar Italian foods served in the United States—macaroni, spaghetti, and pizza—are southern Italian foods introduced by the immigrants from Naples.

Pasta shapes used by Italian cooks also differ from areas in the north to areas in the south. Cooks from northern regions commonly use pastas that are flat ribbons such as fettuccine or linguine, but cooks from southern regions use more tubular pastas such as rigatoni or mostaccioli.

The foods of Italy also vary from region to region. The 20 regions of Italy were independent states until 1861 when Italy was united. This explains how each region developed its own unique culture, traditions, and foods, which are still evident today.

Lamb Chops and Sautéed Peppers

8 lamb rib chops *or* **4 pork rib chops, cut 1 inch thick**

● Place chops on the rack of an unheated broiler pan. Broil 3 inches from the heat, turning once. Broil lamb 10 to 12 minutes or till medium done; broil pork 15 to 18 minutes or till no pink remains. Transfer to a platter.

3 green, sweet red, *or* **yellow peppers, cut into 1-inch pieces**
2 cloves garlic, minced
2 bay leaves
1 teaspoon dried oregano, crushed
2 tablespoons olive oil *or* **cooking oil**

● Meanwhile, in a large skillet cook peppers, garlic, bay leaves, and oregano in hot oil for 12 to 15 minutes or till peppers are crisp-tender. Discard bay leaves. With a slotted spoon transfer peppers to the platter with the chops. Reserve any remaining drippings in the skillet.

¼ cup sliced pitted green *or* **ripe olives**
2 tablespoons snipped parsley
3 anchovy fillets, halved (optional)

● Add olives and parsley to the skillet. If desired, add anchovies. Cook and stir till heated through. Spoon over chops. Serves 4.

Nutrition information per serving: 281 calories, 23 g protein, 4 g carbohydrate, 19 g fat (6 g saturated), 75 mg cholesterol, 285 mg sodium, 401 mg potassium.

Spring Dinner

Lamb is popular in Italy year-round, but it's especially so during spring and the Easter season.

To celebrate spring, Easter, a graduation, or any occasion, invite friends for a dinner party. The following menu designed for eight doesn't require too much last-minute preparation, so you'll have time to enjoy your guests. (Plan on doubling the recipe for Pasta Smothered with Onions and completing the first step of browning the onions before the guests arrive.)

Menu

Consommé

Seasoned Roast Lamb

(see recipe, page 41)

Pasta Smothered with Onions

(see recipe, page 5)

Buttered asparagus

Mixed green salad

Hard rolls

Classic Ricotta Cheesecake

(see recipe, page 118)

Valpolicella or other white wine

**Pasta Smothered
with Onions**
(see recipe, page 5)

Seasoned Roast Lamb

Seasoned Roast Lamb

Arrange asparagus spears, carrot curls, and rosemary sprigs on the platter around the lamb.

1 **4- to 5-pound leg of lamb, beef rib roast, *or* pork center loin roast**
3 **cloves garlic, cut in slivers**
1 **tablespoon olive oil**
1 **tablespoon snipped fresh rosemary *or* 1 teaspoon dried rosemary, crushed**
¼ **teaspoon salt**
¼ **teaspoon pepper**

● Remove fell (paper-thin, pinkish red layer) from outer surface of lamb. Trim fat from lamb, beef, or pork roast.
  Cut small slits in meat and insert garlic. Brush with oil. Rub top of meat with mixture of rosemary, salt, and pepper. Place meat on a rack in a shallow roasting pan. Insert meat thermometer into thickest portion of meat. Roast, uncovered, in a 325° oven. For lamb or beef, allow 1½ to 2 hours or till thermometer registers 140°; for pork, allow 2¼ to 3 hours or till thermometer registers 170°. Remove meat from pan; cover to keep warm.

½ **cup dry white wine, dry vermouth, chicken broth, *or* beef broth**

● For sauce, add wine or broth to pan juices, stirring to scrape up browned bits. Transfer to a small saucepan. Boil gently, uncovered, about 5 minutes or till slightly thickened. Skim off fat.

2 **tablespoons grated Parmesan cheese**
1 **tablespoon snipped parsley**

● Combine Parmesan cheese and parsley. Sprinkle over meat. Pass sauce with meat. Makes 8 to 10 servings.

Nutrition information per serving: 232 calories, 31 g protein, 1 g carbohydrate, 11 g fat (4 g saturated), 96 mg cholesterol, 164 mg sodium, 380 mg potassium.

Turkey Piccata

3 **tablespoons all-purpose flour**
¼ **teaspoon salt**
¾ **pound turkey breast slices (about ¼ inch thick)**
2 **tablespoons margarine *or* butter**

● Combine flour and salt. Rinse turkey; pat dry. Coat with flour mixture. In a large skillet cook turkey in margarine over medium heat 1 to 2 minutes on each side or till tender and no pink remains. Remove from skillet; cover.

2 **tablespoons lemon juice**
1 **tablespoon margarine *or* butter**
1 **tablespoon snipped parsley**

● For sauce, add lemon juice, margarine or butter, and parsley to the skillet. Heat till margarine melts, scraping up browned bits. Pour sauce over turkey. Makes 4 servings.

Nutrition information per serving: 211 calories, 22 g protein, 5 g carbohydrate, 11 g fat (2 g saturated), 49 mg cholesterol, 279 mg sodium, 240 mg potassium.

Pepper-Stuffed Turkey Rolls

For easy entertaining, assemble the rolls early in the day and chill till time to bake.

1 medium green pepper, quartered and seeded
1 medium sweet red pepper, quartered and seeded

● Place peppers, cut side down, on a foil-lined baking sheet. Bake in a 425° oven for 20 to 25 minutes or till skin is bubbly and browned. (*Or,* place pepper pieces, cut side down, on the unheated rack of a broiler pan. Flatten slightly, splitting as necessary. Broil 3 inches from the heat for 8 to 10 minutes or till the skin is bubbly and browned.)

Place peppers in a *new* brown paper bag; seal and let cool 30 minutes. Peel off skin (see page 104). Cut peppers into ½-inch-wide strips.

1 teaspoon olive oil *or* cooking oil
¼ teaspoon dried Italian seasoning, crushed

● In a medium bowl stir together oil, Italian seasoning, ⅛ teaspoon *salt,* and dash *pepper.* Add pepper strips. Toss to coat.

4 4-ounce turkey breast tenderloin steaks
2 teaspoons olive oil *or* cooking oil
2 tablespoons fine dry bread crumbs

● Rinse turkey; pat dry. Divide pepper strips among turkey steaks. Roll up jelly-roll style, starting from a short side. Secure with wooden toothpicks. Place rolls, seam side down, in a 10x6x2-inch baking dish. Brush with oil and sprinkle with crumbs. Bake in 350° oven about 40 minutes or till tender and no pink remains.

1 tablespoon margarine *or* butter
1 tablespoon all-purpose flour
⅛ teaspoon pepper
¾ cup milk
½ cup grated fresh Romano *or* Parmesan cheese

● For sauce, in a small saucepan melt margarine or butter. Stir in flour and pepper. Add milk all at once. Cook and stir till thickened and bubbly. Cook and stir for 1 minute more. Stir in cheese just till melted. Immediately spoon sauce over turkey. Serves 4.

Nutrition information per serving: 276 calories, 33 g protein, 9 g carbohydrate, 12 g fat (4 g saturated), 90 mg cholesterol, 362 mg sodium, 417 mg potassium.

Pepper-Stuffed Chicken Rolls
4 large boned skinless chicken breast halves

Prepare Pepper-Stuffed Turkey Rolls as directed above, *except* substitute chicken for turkey. Place one breast half, boned side up, between 2 pieces of plastic wrap. Working from the center to edges, pound lightly with the flat side of a meat mallet till about ¼ inch thick. Remove plastic wrap. Repeat with remaining breast halves. Divide pepper strips among chicken. Roll up jelly-roll style, starting from a short side and folding in the long sides. Place, seam side down, in a 10x6x2-inch baking dish. Brush with oil and sprinkle with crumbs. Bake in a 350° oven about 25 minutes or till tender and no pink remains. Continue as above.

Lemon-Herb Chicken

1 2½- to 3-pound broiler-fryer chicken, cut up
⅓ cup lemon juice *or* lime juice
2 tablespoons cooking oil *or* olive oil
2 tablespoons water
2 cloves garlic, minced
1½ teaspoons dried basil, crushed
¾ teaspoon dried tarragon, crushed
¼ teaspoon salt

● Rinse chicken; pat dry. Place chicken pieces in a plastic bag set into a shallow bowl.

For marinade, in a small bowl stir together lemon or lime juice, cooking oil or olive oil, water, garlic, basil, tarragon, salt, and ⅛ teaspoon *pepper*. Pour marinade over chicken. Seal bag and turn to coat chicken. Marinate in the refrigerator for 1 hour, turning bag often.

● Drain chicken, reserving marinade. Place chicken, skin side down, on the unheated rack of a broiler pan. Broil 4 to 5 inches from the heat for 20 minutes, brushing often with the reserved marinade. Turn chicken pieces over.

Broil for 5 to 15 minutes more or till tender and no pink remains, brushing with marinade occasionally. Makes 6 servings.

Nutrition information per serving: 226 calories, 28 g protein, 2 g carbohydrate, 12 g fat (3 g saturated), 84 mg cholesterol, 170 mg sodium, 266 mg potassium.

Chicken Cacciatore

Ladle the thick sauce over hot orzo or rosamarina, spaghetti, or rice.

1½ pounds meaty chicken pieces, skinned
1 medium onion, sliced
2 cloves garlic, minced
1 tablespoon cooking oil

● Rinse chicken; pat dry. In a large skillet cook onion and garlic in hot oil till tender. With a slotted spoon, remove onion and garlic from the skillet. In the same skillet cook chicken over medium-high heat about 15 minutes or till lightly browned, turning to brown evenly. Drain off fat. Return onion and garlic to the skillet.

1 14½-ounce can whole Italian-style tomatoes, cut up
1 medium green pepper, cut into 1-inch pieces
½ of a 6-ounce can (⅓ cup) tomato paste
1 2½-ounce jar sliced mushrooms, drained
¼ cup dry red wine
1 or 2 bay leaves
1½ teaspoons dried basil, crushed
1 teaspoon sugar
¼ teaspoon dried rosemary, crushed

● For sauce, in a medium mixing bowl stir together the *undrained* tomatoes, green pepper, tomato paste, mushrooms, wine, bay leaves, basil, sugar, rosemary, ½ teaspoon *salt*, and ¼ teaspoon *pepper*.

Pour sauce over chicken pieces in the skillet. Bring to boiling. Reduce heat. Cover and simmer for 30 to 35 minutes or till chicken is tender and no pink remains. Skim off fat. Discard bay leaves. Makes 4 servings.

Nutrition information per serving: 302 calories, 36 g protein, 13 g carbohydrate, 11 g fat (2 g saturated), 101 mg cholesterol, 604 mg sodium, 828 mg potassium.

Italian Fried Chicken

Sports a tangy, crisp coating of Parmesan or Romano cheese.

1 beaten egg
2 tablespoons water
⅓ cup grated Parmesan *or* Romano cheese
3 tablespoons all-purpose flour
¾ teaspoon dried basil *or* oregano, crushed
Dash pepper

● In a shallow bowl stir together the egg and water. On a sheet of waxed paper, mix together the Parmesan or Romano cheese, flour, basil or oregano, and pepper.

2 pounds meaty chicken pieces
2 tablespoons cooking oil

● If desired, skin chicken pieces. Rinse chicken; pat dry. Dip chicken pieces in egg mixture, then coat with cheese mixture.

In a 12-inch skillet heat oil. Add chicken pieces. Cook, uncovered, over medium-low heat for 50 to 60 minutes or till tender and no pink remains, turning pieces occasionally to brown evenly. Remove chicken and drain on paper towels. Makes 4 servings.

Nutrition information per serving: 336 calories, 33 g protein, 5 g carbohydrate, 20 g fat (5 g saturated), 146 mg cholesterol, 220 mg sodium, 258 mg potassium.

Italian Oven-Fried Chicken

Prepare Italian Fried Chicken as directed above, *except* after coating chicken, arrange pieces, skin side up, in a shallow baking pan so pieces don't touch. Drizzle with the cooking oil. Bake, uncovered, in a 375° oven for 45 to 55 minutes or till tender and no pink remains.

Italian Fried Turkey
4 4-ounce turkey breast tenderloin steaks

Prepare Italian Fried Chicken as directed above, *except* substitute turkey for the chicken. Cook coated turkey in hot oil over medium heat for 10 to 12 minutes or till lightly browned and no pink remains, turning once.

Nutrition information per serving: 265 calories, 35 g protein, 5 g carbohydrate, 11 g fat (3 g saturated), 142 mg cholesterol, 192 mg sodium, 312 mg potassium.

Cheese-Stuffed Chicken Breasts

A wonderful blend of ricotta, fontina, and Romano cheeses plus mushrooms accents the baked chicken breasts.

½ **cup finely chopped fresh mushrooms**
1 **tablespoon margarine *or* butter**

● In a medium skillet cook mushrooms in hot margarine or butter till tender. Remove skillet from the heat.

½ **cup ricotta cheese**
½ **cup shredded fontina *or* mozzarella cheese (2 ounces)**
¼ **cup grated Romano *or* Parmesan cheese**
¼ **cup snipped parsley**
2 **tablespoons fine dry Italian seasoned bread crumbs**

● Add ricotta cheese, fontina or mozzarella cheese, Romano or Parmesan cheese, parsley, and bread crumbs to mushrooms. Stir gently. Set cheese mixture aside.

2 **whole medium chicken breasts (about 1½ pounds total)**
Paprika

● Rinse chicken; pat dry. Bone and halve chicken breasts, *leaving skin attached.* Stuff about ⅓ *cup* of the cheese mixture between the skin and flesh of *each* breast half. Place chicken, skin side up, in a 9x9x2-inch baking pan. Sprinkle with paprika.

Bake, uncovered, in a 350° oven for 25 to 30 minutes or till chicken is tender and no pink remains. Makes 4 servings.

Nutrition information per serving: 370 calories, 39 g protein, 4 g carbohydrate, 21 g fat (9 g saturated), 122 mg cholesterol, 238 mg sodium, 353 mg potassium.

Beginning on one of the long sides, gently loosen the skin from the chicken breast half, leaving the skin attached at the other side. Then, spoon the cheese mixture between the flesh and the skin.

Crispy Gnocchi
(see recipe, page 97)

Skillet Chicken and Vegetables

Skillet Chicken and Vegetables

1½ **pounds meaty chicken pieces**
1 **large leek, sliced**
1 **cup sliced fresh mushrooms**
2 **cloves garlic, minced**
1½ **teaspoons dried Italian seasoning, crushed**
2 **tablespoons cooking oil**

● If desired, skin chicken. Rinse chicken; pat dry. Sprinkle chicken with *salt* and *pepper.*
  In a large skillet cook leek, mushrooms, garlic, and Italian seasoning in hot oil till leek is tender. Add chicken pieces to the skillet and cook over medium heat for 10 minutes, turning to brown evenly.

1 **cup chicken broth**
½ **cup sun-dried tomatoes (oil pack), coarsely snipped**

● Add broth and tomatoes to the skillet. Bring to boiling. Reduce heat. Cover and simmer for 20 minutes.

1 **9-ounce package frozen artichoke hearts**
2 **tablespoons water**
4 **teaspoons cornstarch**

● Meanwhile, thaw artichokes enough to separate. Halve any large artichokes, then add to the skillet. Simmer, covered, for 10 to 15 minutes or till chicken is tender and no pink remains. Transfer chicken and vegetables from the skillet to a platter. Cover to keep warm.
  Skim off any fat from sauce in skillet. Stir together water and cornstarch. Add to skillet. Cook and stir till thickened and bubbly. Cook and stir for 2 minutes more. Serve sauce with chicken and vegetables. Makes 4 servings.

Nutrition information per serving: 406 calories, 30 g protein, 26 g carbohydrate, 22 g fat (4 g saturated), 76 mg cholesterol, 322 mg sodium, 1,082 mg potassium.

Chicken Livers with Sage

Ready to serve in only 20 minutes.

1 **medium onion, cut into thin wedges**
2 **tablespoons margarine *or* butter**
1 **pound chicken livers, cut in half**
2 **teaspoons snipped fresh sage *or***
    ½ **teaspoon dried sage, crushed**
⅛ **teaspoon salt**

● In a large skillet cook onion in margarine or butter till tender but not brown. Stir in chicken livers, sage, salt, and ⅛ teaspoon *pepper.* Cook, covered, over medium heat about 5 minutes or till centers of livers are only slightly pink, stirring occasionally.

¼ **cup dry marsala *or* chicken broth**
½ **teaspoon cornstarch**
4 **slices Baked, Fried, *or* Broiled Polenta (see recipes, page 93) *or* Italian bread, toasted**
1 **tablespoon snipped parsley**

● In a small bowl stir together marsala or broth and cornstarch. Add to livers in the skillet. Cook and stir over medium heat till thickened and bubbly. Cook and stir for 2 minutes more. Serve liver mixture over Polenta or toasted bread. Sprinkle with parsley. Makes 4 servings.

Nutrition information per serving: 287 calories, 23 g protein, 21 g carbohydrate, 11 g fat (3 g saturated), 536 mg cholesterol, 535 mg sodium, 197 mg potassium.

FISH & SHELLFISH

Because their country is surrounded by the sea on three sides,

Italians have always enjoyed a wide variety of fish

and shellfish. Turn the page and find inviting ways of

preparing fish and shellfish, from baking fresh

fish fillets in cream to marinating and grilling shellfish.

Haddock Baked in Cream

Perfect for a special dinner—rich and elegant, yet easy to make.

1 pound fresh *or* frozen haddock *or* cod fillets (½ to ¾ inch thick)
½ cup whipping cream
¼ cup sliced green onion
¼ cup snipped parsley
2 tablespoons grated Parmesan cheese
2 tablespoons dry white wine
1 clove garlic, minced
¼ teaspoon salt
Dash pepper

● Thaw fish, if frozen. Remove any skin. Cut into 4 serving-size portions. Place fish in an 11x7x1½- or 9x9x2-inch baking pan. In a small bowl stir together whipping cream, onion, parsley, Parmesan cheese, wine, garlic, salt, and pepper. Pour cream mixture over fish. Bake, uncovered, in a 350° oven for 20 to 25 minutes or till fish flakes easily with a fork.

1 tablespoon grated Parmesan cheese

● Place fish on a serving platter with sides or in individual au gratin dishes. With a wire whisk, stir sauce to blend. Pour sauce over fish. Sprinkle with Parmesan cheese. Serves 4.

Nutrition information per serving: 227 calories, 25 g protein, 2 g carbohydrate, 13 g fat (8 g saturated), 107 mg cholesterol, 291 mg sodium, 410 mg potassium.

Baked Swordfish with Fennel

If fresh fennel isn't available, substitute about 1½ cups chopped celery.

1 pound fresh *or* frozen swordfish, shark, *or* tuna steaks, cut 1 inch thick

● Thaw fish, if frozen. Cut into 4 serving-size portions. Set aside.

1 fennel *or* anise bulb (about 1 pound)
¼ cup dry white wine
2 tablespoons snipped parsley
⅛ teaspoon crushed red pepper
1½ cups Chunky Vegetable Sauce (see recipe, page 10) *or* purchased garden-style spaghetti sauce

● For sauce, cut fennel into thin wedges. In a medium saucepan combine fennel, wine, parsley, and red pepper. Bring to boiling. Reduce heat. Cover and simmer about 10 minutes or till fennel is almost tender. Stir in Chunky Vegetable Sauce or spaghetti sauce. Pour mixture into a 10x6x2-inch baking dish.

Salt
Pepper
1 tablespoon lemon juice
4 ounces packaged orzo or rosamarina *or* other pasta, cooked and drained (see chart, page 8)

● Lightly sprinkle fish with salt and pepper. Arrange fish on top of sauce in the baking dish. Drizzle fish with lemon juice.
　　Bake, covered, in a 350° oven for 40 to 45 minutes or till fish flakes easily with a fork. Transfer fish to a platter. Spoon sauce over fish. Serve with hot orzo. Makes 4 servings.

Nutrition information per serving: 356 calories, 28 g protein, 38 g carbohydrate, 9 g fat (2 g saturated), 43 mg cholesterol, 400 mg sodium, 914 mg potassium.

Mini Italian Loaves
(see recipe, page 84)

Ricotta-Stuffed Flounder

Chunky Vegetable Sauce
(see recipe, page 10)

Ricotta-Stuffed Flounder

1 pound fresh *or* frozen flounder *or* sole fillets
1 cup ½-inch bread cubes

● Thaw fish, if frozen. Spread bread cubes in a shallow baking pan. Bake in a 350° oven about 10 minutes or till dry, stirring twice.

¼ cup shredded carrot
¼ cup shredded zucchini
¼ cup thinly sliced green onion
1 tablespoon cooking oil
¾ cup ricotta cheese
2 tablespoons grated Parmesan cheese
2 tablespoons snipped parsley
1 teaspoon dried Italian seasoning, crushed
⅛ teaspoon pepper

● In a medium skillet cook carrot, zucchini, and onion in hot oil till tender. Remove from the heat. Stir in ricotta, Parmesan cheese, parsley, Italian seasoning, and pepper. Add ¾ cup of the dry bread cubes. Toss gently.

Divide fish into 6 portions. Arrange fillets around the edges of six 6-ounce custard cups, leaving centers open. Spoon about ¼ cup of the ricotta mixture into *each* center. Place cups in a shallow baking pan. Bake, covered, in a 375° oven for 10 minutes. Uncover; bake about 15 minutes more or till fish flakes easily with a fork. Let stand 5 minutes.

1 cup Chunky Vegetable Sauce (see recipe, page 10) *or* purchased garden-style spaghetti sauce

● In a small saucepan heat sauce. Spoon *2 to 3 tablespoons* of the sauce onto *each* dinner plate. Carefully remove fish from custard cups and place on top of the sauce. Serves 6.

Nutrition information per serving: 205 calories, 19 g protein, 10 g carbohydrate, 10 g fat (4 g saturated), 56 mg cholesterol, 238 mg sodium, 430 mg potassium.

Flounder Bundles

Tucked inside each bundle is a perfectly baked fillet spiked with pesto and shallots.

4 4-ounce fresh *or* frozen flounder *or* sole fillets (about ½ inch thick)

● Thaw fish, if frozen. Place each fish fillet on a 9x9-inch piece of heavy foil or parchment paper. Fold each fillet crosswise in half.

2 tablespoons lemon juice
2 tablespoons finely chopped shallots
1 small clove garlic, minced
⅛ teaspoon pepper
¼ cup Pesto (see recipe, page 16)

● In a small bowl stir together lemon juice, shallots, garlic, and pepper. Spoon evenly over fish. Spoon Pesto evenly over fish. Seal each square of foil or paper by folding the edges together. Place in a 15x10x1-inch baking pan.

Bake in a 400° oven about 15 minutes or till bundles puff slightly and fish flakes easily with a fork (*carefully* open bundles to check doneness). Makes 4 servings.

Nutrition information per serving: 152 calories, 20 g protein, 3 g carbohydrate, 7 g fat (2 g saturated), 51 mg cholesterol, 193 mg sodium, 336 mg potassium.

Fillets Florentine

Spinach-filled fish plus Parmesan cheese sauce and almonds equals one terrific dish.

1½ **pounds fresh *or* frozen flounder, cod, *or* sole fillets (½ to 1 inch thick)** 1 **10-ounce package frozen chopped spinach, cooked** ¾ **cup ricotta cheese *or* small curd cottage cheese, drained** ½ **teaspoon dried basil, crushed**	● Thaw fish, if frozen. Drain cooked spinach, pressing out excess water. In a medium bowl stir together spinach, ricotta cheese or cottage cheese, and basil. Set aside.
1½ **cups water**	● Measure thickness of fish. Cut large fillets crosswise in half. In a large skillet bring water to boiling. Carefully add fish. Return just to boiling. Reduce heat. Cover and simmer till fish flakes easily with a fork (allow 4 to 6 minutes per ½-inch thickness of fish). With a slotted spoon remove fish from the skillet. Place *half* of the fish in an 8x8x2-inch broilerproof baking dish. Spoon spinach mixture on top of fish in the baking dish. Top with remaining fish.

1 **tablespoon margarine *or* butter**
1 **tablespoon all-purpose flour**
   Dash salt
   Dash pepper
½ **cup milk**
2 **tablespoons grated *or* finely shredded Parmesan cheese**
2 **tablespoons dry white wine**
½ **teaspoon lemon juice**
	● In a small saucepan melt margarine or butter. Stir in flour, salt, and pepper. Add milk all at once. Cook and stir till thickened and bubbly. Stir in Parmesan cheese, wine, and lemon juice. Pour over fish.

2 **tablespoons grated *or* finely shredded Parmesan cheese** 2 **tablespoons sliced almonds**	● Sprinkle Parmesan cheese and almonds on the fish. Broil 4 to 5 inches from the heat for 2 to 3 minutes or till lightly browned and heated through. Makes 6 servings.

Nutrition information per serving: 228 calories, 28 g protein, 6 g carbohydrate, 10 g fat (4 g saturated), 78 mg cholesterol, 273 mg sodium, 525 mg potassium.

Marsala-Marinated Trout

**4 8- to 10-ounce fresh *or* frozen pan-
    dressed rainbow trout *or* lake perch**
½ cup dry marsala *or* other white wine
1 tablespoon lemon juice
½ teaspoon dried thyme, crushed

● Thaw fish, if frozen. Place fish in a shallow baking dish. Sprinkle with *salt* and *pepper.*
    For marinade, stir together marsala, lemon juice, and thyme; pour over fish. Cover and marinate in the refrigerator for 2 hours. Drain fish, reserving marinade. Pat fish dry.

½ cup sliced fresh mushrooms
1 medium carrot, chopped (½ cup)
1 small onion, chopped (⅓ cup)
1 clove garlic, minced
2 tablespoons cooking oil
¼ cup chicken broth

● In a 12-inch skillet cook mushrooms, carrot, onion, and garlic in hot oil till tender but not brown. Push to the edges of the skillet. Add fish and cook 4 minutes on each side. Add marinade and broth. Cover and simmer about 4 minutes or till fish flakes easily with a fork. Transfer fish and vegetables to a platter; cover.
    Simmer marinade mixture till reduced to ¼ *cup;* spoon over fish. Makes 4 servings.

Nutrition information per serving: 263 calories, 31 g protein, 4 g carbohydrate, 12 g fat (2 g saturated), 83 mg cholesterol, 95 mg sodium, 870 mg potassium.

Fish Frittata

When you're in a hurry, you don't even need to thaw the fish.

**½ pound fresh *or* frozen fish fillets
    (about ½ inch thick)**
½ cup chopped onion
½ cup chopped zucchini
2 tablespoons cooking oil

● In a large broilerproof skillet, bring ½ inch water to boiling. Add fresh or frozen fish. Simmer, covered, for 4 to 6 minutes for fresh fish or 6 to 9 minutes for frozen fish, or till fish flakes easily. Drain. Flake fish into bite-size pieces; set aside. Wipe skillet dry. In the skillet cook onion and zucchini in hot oil till tender.

6 beaten eggs
¼ teaspoon salt
¼ teaspoon dried tarragon, crushed
¼ teaspoon pepper
**1 cup Chunky Vegetable Sauce
    (see recipe, page 10) *or* purchased
    garden-style spaghetti sauce,
    warmed**

● In a medium bowl stir together eggs, salt, tarragon, and pepper. Stir in fish. Pour egg mixture into the skillet over vegetables. Cook over medium-low heat. As mixture sets, run a spatula around edge of skillet, lifting egg mixture to allow uncooked portion to flow underneath. Continue cooking and lifting edges till mixture is almost set (surface will be moist).
    Place skillet under the broiler 5 inches from the heat. Broil for 1 to 2 minutes or till top is just set. Cut into wedges. Serve with warm vegetable or spaghetti sauce. Serves 4.

Nutrition information per serving: 275 calories, 20 g protein, 9 g carbohydrate, 18 g fat (4 g saturated), 343 mg cholesterol, 383 mg sodium, 391 mg potassium.

Stir-Fried Tuna and Vegetables

Choose either tuna or swordfish steaks.

1 pound fresh *or* frozen tuna steaks *or* swordfish steaks, cut ¾ inch thick

● Thaw fish, if frozen. Cut fish steaks into 1-inch pieces. Set aside.

¾ cup water
¼ cup dry white wine
4 teaspoons cornstarch
2 teaspoons instant chicken bouillon granules
½ teaspoon dried thyme, crushed

● In a small bowl stir together water, wine, cornstarch, chicken bouillon granules, and thyme. Set aside.

1 tablespoon cooking oil
2 cloves garlic, minced
½ cup thinly sliced carrot
1 9-ounce package frozen Italian-style green beans, thawed

● Preheat a wok or large skillet over high heat; add oil. Stir-fry garlic in hot oil for 15 seconds. Add carrot, and stir-fry for 2 minutes.
   Add thawed beans, and stir-fry for 2 to 3 minutes or till vegetables are crisp-tender. Remove vegetables from the wok or skillet.

Cooking oil (optional)
1 medium tomato, cut into thin wedges

● If necessary, add more oil to the wok or skillet. Add *half* of the fish to the wok or skillet. Stir-fry for 3 to 5 minutes or till fish flakes easily with a fork, being careful not to break up pieces. Remove from the wok or skillet. Repeat with remaining fish.
   Return all fish to the wok or skillet. Push fish to edges of the wok or skillet. Stir wine mixture and add to the center of the wok or skillet. Cook and stir till thickened and bubbly. Stir in vegetables and tomato. Cook 1 minute more.

2 tablespoons pine nuts *or* chopped walnuts, toasted
4 ounces packaged orzo or rosamarina *or* ⅔ cup rice, cooked and drained (see chart, page 8)

● Transfer fish and vegetable mixture to a warm serving bowl. Sprinkle with nuts. Serve with hot cooked orzo or rice. Makes 4 servings.

Nutrition information per serving: 344 calories, 34 g protein, 34 g carbohydrate, 7 g fat (1 g saturated), 51 mg cholesterol, 510 mg sodium, 659 mg potassium.

Lemon-Basil Grilled Swordfish

Toss sprigs of basil or oregano on the coals to give the fish extra flavor.

**1 pound fresh *or* frozen swordfish,
  salmon, *or* halibut steaks *or* fillets**
½ cup dry white wine
½ teaspoon finely shredded lemon peel
2 tablespoons lemon juice
2 tablespoons olive oil *or* cooking oil
1 tablespoon snipped parsley
**1 tablespoon snipped fresh basil *or*
  oregano, *or* 1 teaspoon dried basil
  or oregano, crushed**

● Thaw fish, if frozen. Cut fish into 4 serving-size portions. Place in a shallow baking dish.

For marinade, in a small bowl stir together wine, lemon peel, lemon juice, olive oil or cooking oil, parsley, and basil or oregano. Pour marinade over fish. Cover and marinate in the refrigerator for 1 to 2 hours, turning fish over occasionally.

**3 or 4 sprigs fresh basil *or* oregano
  Lemon wedges**

● Drain fish, reserving marinade. Measure thickness of fish. Place herb sprigs directly on *medium-hot* coals. Place fish in a greased grill basket or on a grill rack. Grill on an uncovered grill directly over the coals for 4 to 6 minutes per ½-inch thickness or till fish flakes easily, turning once and brushing with marinade 2 or 3 times. Serve with lemon. Makes 4 servings.

Nutrition information per serving: 211 calories, 22 g protein, 2 g carbohydrate, 11 g fat (2 g saturated), 43 mg cholesterol, 100 mg sodium, 370 mg potassium.

Italian Wines

No Italian lunch or dinner would be complete without a wine. Following are just a few of the more popular Italian wines:

● *Asti Spumante* is a sparkling white wine. Its fruity flavor is great with desserts.
● *Barbaresco,* a red wine with a brownish color, is full-bodied. Serve it with beef, veal, and cheese.
● *Bardolino,* a light red wine, has a delicate, dry flavor. Serve it with fish, veal, and poultry.
● *Barola* is a popular red wine with a smooth, deep flavor. Serve it with meat, game, and strong cheeses.
● *Chianti* is a dry red wine with a warm fruity flavor. It goes with most foods.

● *Lambrusco,* a bubbly red wine, ranges from dry to slightly sweet. Its fruity flavor is best when slightly chilled.
● *Marsala* is similar to sherry, with an amber color. It is available both sweet and dry. Serve it as an aperitif or a dessert wine, or use it for cooking.
● *Orvieto* is a fruity white wine that comes dry or semisweet. Serve it with antipasto or dessert.
● *Soave,* a dry white wine, has a mild, delicate flavor. Serve it chilled with antipasto, fish, or poultry.
● *Valpolicella* is a dry to slightly sweet red wine with a mellow flavor. Serve it with antipasto, beef, lamb, cheese, or dessert.
● *Verdicchio* is a dry white wine with a fresh taste that goes well with fish.

Broiled Halibut

A hint of rosemary and garlic flavors the crisp coating.

1 pound fresh *or* frozen halibut *or* swordfish steaks, cut ¾ inch thick

● Thaw fish, if frozen. Cut into 4 serving-size portions. Rinse fish steak portions and pat dry with paper towels.

2 tablespoons lemon juice
1 tablespoon cooking oil
1 clove garlic, minced
⅓ cup fine dry bread crumbs
½ teaspoon dried rosemary, crushed

● Stir together lemon juice, oil, and garlic; brush on both sides of fish steaks. On a sheet of waxed paper, combine bread crumbs and rosemary. Dip fish in crumb mixture to coat both sides. Place fish on a plate. Cover and chill for 30 to 60 minutes.

1 lemon, cut into wedges, *or* ¼ cup Pesto (see recipe, page 16)

● Place fish on the greased unheated rack of a broiler pan. Broil 4 inches from the heat for 6 to 9 minutes or till fish flakes easily with a fork, turning once. Serve lemon wedges or Pesto with fish steaks. Makes 4 servings.

Nutrition information per serving: 187 calories, 24 g protein, 8 g carbohydrate, 6 g fat (1 g saturated), 1 mg cholesterol, 120 mg sodium, 526 mg potassium.

Parmesan Fish

1 pound fresh *or* frozen cod, orange roughy, haddock, *or* other fish fillets (½ to ¾ inch thick)
2 tablespoons fine dry bread crumbs
2 tablespoons grated Parmesan cheese
1 teaspoon snipped parsley
⅛ teaspoon dried basil *or* oregano, crushed
⅛ teaspoon pepper

● Thaw fish, if frozen. Cut fish into 4 serving-size portions.
  In a small bowl stir together bread crumbs, Parmesan cheese, parsley, basil or oregano, and pepper. Set crumb mixture aside.

1 tablespoon lemon juice
Lemon wedges

● Place fish on the greased unheated rack of a broiler pan. Brush with lemon juice. Broil 5 to 6 inches from the heat for 3 minutes.
  Sprinkle crumb mixture over fish. Broil 3 to 6 minutes more or till fish flakes easily with a fork. Serve lemon wedges with fish. Serves 4.

Nutrition information per serving: 116 calories, 21 g protein, 3 g carbohydrate, 2 g fat (1 g saturated), 49 mg cholesterol, 137 mg sodium, 234 mg potassium.

Broiled Halibut

Marinated Vegetable Salad
(see recipe, page 105)

Fried Soft-Shell Blue Crabs

This dish also makes an impressive appetizer for eight people.

4 large *or* 8 small soft-shell blue crabs (10 to 12 ounces total)

● Handling crabs carefully, grasp each crab between the back legs. Using kitchen shears, cut across the body about ½ inch behind the eyes, removing the face.

Lift the pointed soft top shell on one side. Using your fingers, push up the "devil's fingers" (the spongy projectiles on the exposed side), and pull off. Replace the soft top shell over the body. Repeat on the other side.

Turn crab over. Pull up the apron-shaped piece; discard. Thoroughly rinse crab under cold running water to remove the mustard-colored substance. Pat dry.

1 beaten egg
1 tablespoon water
½ cup finely crushed saltine crackers
⅓ cup ground walnuts
2 tablespoons all-purpose flour
¼ teaspoon dried tarragon, crushed
¼ cup cooking oil
Lemon wedges

● In a shallow dish stir together egg and water. On a sheet of waxed paper combine crackers, nuts, flour, and tarragon. Dip crabs in egg mixture, then roll in cracker mixture.

In a large skillet heat oil. Add *half* of the crabs, back side down. Fry for 6 to 10 minutes or till golden and crisp, carefully turning once. Drain on paper towels. Keep warm in a 300° oven. Repeat with remaining crabs, adding more oil, if necessary. Serve warm with lemon wedges. Makes 4 servings.

Nutrition information per serving: 319 calories, 15 g protein, 13 g carbohydrate, 23 g fat (3 g saturated), 113 mg cholesterol, 310 mg sodium, 254 mg potassium.

Spinach-Stuffed Squid

Many fish markets and large supermarkets carry squid that is already cleaned.

2 pounds fresh *or* frozen medium squid (with bodies about 5 inches long)

● Thaw squid, if frozen. To clean, pull head and tentacles out of the body. Cut the head off the tentacles. Reserve tentacles; discard head.

Remove and discard any entrails that remain in the body. Pull out and discard the clear cartilage "pen" running down the back of the body. With your fingers, peel skin off outside of the body, leaving body whole. Rinse body and tentacles; pat dry.

1 10-ounce package frozen chopped spinach, thawed
Nonstick spray coating
1 tablespoon finely chopped onion
1 clove garlic, minced
⅓ cup cooked rice
2 tablespoons snipped fresh basil *or* 2 teaspoons dried basil, crushed

● Drain spinach, pressing out excess water. Spray a cold large skillet with nonstick coating. Add onion and garlic; cook over medium heat till tender but not brown. Remove from the heat.

Stir in spinach, rice, and basil. Fill each squid ½ to ⅔ full. (Do not overfill or the squid may split while cooking.)

2 tablespoons olive oil *or* cooking oil
1 8-ounce can stewed tomatoes

● Wipe out the skillet with paper towels. In the skillet heat oil over medium heat. Add stuffed squid and tentacles. Cook about 5 minutes or till browned, turning to brown all sides.

Add tomatoes. Bring to boiling. Reduce heat. Cover and simmer for 30 to 40 minutes or till squid are tender, turning squid once. Transfer squid and vegetables to a serving platter. Discard cooking liquid. Makes 4 servings.

Nutrition information per serving: 286 calories, 33 g protein, 18 g carbohydrate, 10 g fat (2 g saturated), 429 mg cholesterol, 294 mg sodium, 702 mg potassium.

Holding the squid's body in one hand, firmly grasp the tentacles with the other hand. Then, pull the tentacles, head, and entrails out of the body.

Crumb-Topped Lobster Tails

4 frozen lobster tails (about 6 ounces each)

● Partially thaw lobster tails. Rinse and pat dry. To butterfly tails, use kitchen shears or a sharp heavy knife to cut lengthwise through centers of hard top shells and meat, cutting to, *but not through,* bottom shells. Using fingers, press shell halves apart. Place lobster tails, bottom-shell side down, on the unheated rack of a broiler pan. Broil 4 to 6 inches from the heat 10 to 11 minutes or till meat is *just* opaque.

¼ cup fine dry bread crumbs
2 tablespoons grated Parmesan *or* Romano cheese
1 tablespoon snipped parsley
½ teaspoon dried oregano, crushed
¼ teaspoon garlic powder
⅛ teaspoon ground red pepper
2 tablespoons margarine *or* butter, melted

● Meanwhile, stir together bread crumbs, Parmesan or Romano cheese, parsley, oregano, garlic powder, and red pepper. Add melted margarine and toss together. Sprinkle crumb mixture over lobster meat. Broil 1 to 2 minutes more or till crumbs are golden. Serves 4.

Nutrition information per serving: 171 calories, 19 g protein, 6 g carbohydrate, 7 g fat (2 g saturated), 63 mg cholesterol, 484 mg sodium, 324 mg potassium.

Shrimp and Artichoke Frittata

Serve for a light supper or a brunch with white wine and a loaf of Italian bread.

½ of a 9-ounce package frozen artichoke hearts
¼ cup chopped onion
1 clove garlic, minced
2 tablespoons margarine *or* butter

● Cook artichokes according to package directions. Drain; cut hearts in half. Set aside.
In a large broilerproof skillet, cook onion and garlic in hot margarine or butter till onion is tender but not brown. Remove from the heat.

6 beaten eggs
1 4½-ounce can shrimp, rinsed and drained
⅛ teaspoon pepper

● In a bowl stir together eggs, shrimp, and pepper. Pour over onion in the skillet. Cook over medium-low heat. As egg mixture sets, run a spatula around the edge of the skillet, lifting egg mixture to allow uncooked portion to flow underneath. Continue cooking and lifting edges till mixture is almost set (surface will be moist).

2 tablespoons grated fresh Parmesan cheese

● Place skillet under the broiler 5 inches from heat. Broil for 1 to 2 minutes or till top is just set. Distribute artichokes evenly over top and sprinkle with Parmesan cheese. Broil for 1 minute more. Loosen bottom of frittata and slide onto a plate. Cut into wedges. Serves 4.

Nutrition information per serving: 228 calories, 18 g protein, 5 g carbohydrate, 15 g fat (4 g saturated), 371 mg cholesterol, 210 mg sodium, 169 mg potassium.

Lemon-Marinated Shrimp

1¼ **pounds fresh *or* frozen large *or* jumbo shrimp in shells**

● Thaw shrimp, if frozen. Peel shrimp, leaving tails intact. Devein shrimp. Rinse and pat dry.

¼ **cup olive oil**
1 **teaspoon finely shredded lemon peel**
2 **tablespoons lemon juice**
2 **cloves garlic, minced**
½ **teaspoon dried oregano, crushed**

● In a large bowl combine olive oil, lemon peel, lemon juice, garlic, oregano, and ⅛ teaspoon *pepper*. Add shrimp; stir well.
 Cover and marinate at room temperature for 1 hour or in the refrigerator for 2 hours. Drain, reserving marinade.

● Place shrimp on the unheated rack of a broiler pan. Broil 4 to 5 inches from the heat about 4 minutes for large or about 6 minutes for jumbo, or till shrimp turn pink, turning and brushing with marinade once. Makes 4 servings.

Nutrition information per serving: 250 calories, 27 g protein, 1 g carbohydrate, 15 g fat (2 g saturated), 249 mg cholesterol, 286 mg sodium, 251 mg potassium.

Dinner Menu

A typical Italian menu, with its many courses, may sound like a heavy meal. However, Italians believe in leaving the table satisfied, never stuffed. They do this by serving small portions.
 Italian meals usually begin with an antipasto followed by a pasta or soup course. Then, the entrée is served. Vegetables and green salad are served either with the entrée or after it. The final course is usually cheese and/or fruit. Desserts are served on special occasions.
 An Italian menu usually has only one wine that is served throughout the meal rather than a different wine with each course.
 This dinner menu is patterned after the Italian style and is sure to please your guests.

Menu

Antipasto platter

Hot cooked pasta

(see recipes, pages 12 and 13)

Lemon-Marinated Shrimp

(see recipe, above)

Spinach salad

Italian bread

Pears with Raspberry Sauce

(see recipe, page 121)

Verdicchio or soave wine

Shrimp with Peppers

1½ cups chopped green, sweet red,
    or yellow peppers
1 cup chopped onion
1 teaspoon dried basil, crushed
1 tablespoon olive oil *or* cooking oil
2 ounces prosciutto *or* fully cooked
    ham, finely chopped

● In a large skillet cook peppers, onion, and basil in hot olive oil or cooking oil till tender but not brown. Stir in prosciutto or ham and cook for 1 minute more.

1 pound fresh shrimp, peeled and
    deveined
2 tablespoons dry marsala *or* other
    white wine
1 tablespoon white wine vinegar
1 teaspoon finely shredded lemon peel
⅛ teaspoon crushed red pepper
    Lemon slices

● Stir shrimp, marsala, vinegar, lemon peel, and red pepper into the skillet. Cover and cook over medium heat 4 to 6 minutes or till shrimp turn pink. Serve with lemon. Makes 4 servings.

Nutrition information per serving: 167 calories, 22 g protein, 6 g carbohydrate, 5 g fat (1 g saturated), 174 mg cholesterol, 382 mg sodium, 364 mg potassium.

Grilled Scallop Kabobs

When it isn't grilling weather, broil the scallop and vegetable kabobs 4 to 5 inches from the heat for the times given.

¾ pound fresh *or* frozen scallops

● Thaw scallops, if frozen. Halve any large ones. Place in a plastic bag set into a dish.

¼ cup olive oil *or* cooking oil
2 tablespoons lime juice *or* lemon juice
1 tablespoon snipped parsley
1 clove garlic, minced
½ teaspoon dried basil, crushed
½ teaspoon dried oregano, crushed

● For marinade, in a small bowl stir together oil, lime or lemon juice, parsley, garlic, basil, oregano, ⅛ teaspoon *salt*, and dash *pepper*.
    Pour marinade over scallops. Seal bag. Marinate in the refrigerator for 3 to 4 hours, turning bag occasionally.

1 medium zucchini, cut into ½-inch
    slices
1 medium green *or* sweet red pepper,
    cut into 1-inch squares
8 fresh mushrooms

● Meanwhile, cook zucchini, pepper, and mushrooms, covered, in a small amount of boiling water for 2 minutes. Drain.
    Drain scallops, reserving marinade. Alternately thread scallops, zucchini, pepper, and mushrooms onto eight 12-inch skewers.

8 cherry tomatoes

● Place skewers on a greased grill rack. Grill on an uncovered grill directly over *medium-hot* coals for 10 to 12 minutes or till scallops are opaque, brushing with marinade and turning occasionally. Add tomatoes to ends of skewers the last 1 minute of cooking. Serves 4.

Nutrition information per serving: 219 calories, 16 g protein, 8 g carbohydrate, 15 g fat (2 g saturated), 28 mg cholesterol, 209 mg sodium, 565 mg potassium.

Shrimp with Peppers

PIZZAS
&
SANDWICHES

Pizza and sandwiches are the mainstays of light Italian meals.

To Americans, pizza is a thick or thin crust piled high

with sauce, toppings, and cheese. But to Italians, pizza is

anything that resembles a pie. Take a look at our

special section called Pizza Toppings, or choose a traditional

Italian-style pizza or a favorite sandwich.

Pizza Margherita

For lots of color, use a yellow and a red tomato.

1 Pizza Crust (see recipe for thin crust, page 66)

● Prebake the thin crust as directed.

1 cup shredded mozzarella cheese (4 ounces)
2 medium ripe fresh tomatoes, thinly sliced
1 tablespoon olive oil
1 tablespoon snipped fresh basil *or* 1 teaspoon dried basil, crushed
¼ cup grated Parmesan cheese

● Sprinkle mozzarella cheese over the prebaked crust. Without overlapping, arrange the tomatoes in a circular pattern on top of the cheese. Drizzle with olive oil. Sprinkle the basil, then the Parmesan cheese over the top. Bake for 10 to 15 minutes more or till bubbly. Serve hot. Makes 4 to 6 side-dish servings.

Nutrition information per serving: 326 calories, 15 g protein, 37 g carbohydrate, 14 g fat (5 g saturated), 20 mg cholesterol, 299 mg sodium, 228 mg potassium.

Pizza Bianca

Even without a tomatoey sauce, it's still considered a pizza.

1 Pizza Crust (see recipe for thin crust, page 66)

● Prebake the thin crust as directed.

1 tablespoon olive oil
1½ cups shredded mozzarella cheese (6 ounces)
¼ cup grated Parmesan *or* Romano cheese
1 tablespoon snipped fresh basil *or* 1 teaspoon dried basil, crushed
¼ teaspoon coarsely ground pepper

● Brush olive oil over the prebaked crust. Sprinkle with mozzarella cheese, Parmesan or Romano cheese, basil, and pepper. Bake for 10 to 15 minutes more or till bubbly. Serve hot. Makes 4 to 6 side-dish servings.

Nutrition information per serving: 367 calories, 18 g protein, 39 g carbohydrate, 16 g fat (6 g saturated), 28 mg cholesterol, 363 mg sodium, 194 mg potassium.

Pizza Crust

One recipe lets you make thick or thin crusts. (Thin crusts are pictured on pages 68 and 69.)

2¾ to 3¼ cups all-purpose flour
1 package active dry yeast
¼ teaspoon salt
1 cup warm water (120° to 130°)
2 tablespoons olive oil *or* cooking oil

● In a large mixing bowl combine *1¼ cups* of the flour, the yeast, and salt. Add water and oil. Beat with an electric mixer on low speed for 30 seconds, scraping the bowl. Beat on high speed for 3 minutes. Stir in as much of the remaining flour as you can. On a lightly floured surface, knead in enough remaining flour to make a moderately stiff dough that is smooth and elastic (6 to 8 minutes total). Divide in half. Cover and let rest 10 minutes.

Cornmeal (optional)

● For *thin crusts,* grease two 12-inch pizza pans or large baking sheets. If desired, sprinkle with cornmeal. Roll each half of the dough into a 13-inch circle. Transfer to prepared pans. Build up edges slightly. *Do not let rise.* Prebake in a 425° oven about 12 minutes or till lightly browned. Add desired toppings (see pages 68 and 69). Bake 10 to 15 minutes or till bubbly.

For *thick crusts,* grease two 11x7x1½-inch or 9x9x2-inch baking pans. If desired, sprinkle with cornmeal. With greased fingers, pat each half into bottom and halfway up sides of prepared pans. Cover; let rise in a warm place till *nearly* double (30 to 45 minutes). Prebake in a 375° oven for 25 to 30 minutes or till lightly browned. Add desired toppings (see pages 68 and 69). Bake 20 to 25 minutes or till bubbly. Let stand 5 minutes before slicing.

Makes 2 thin or thick crusts.

Note: If you need only 1 crust, freeze the extra dough. Form into a ball. Wrap in plastic wrap and transfer to freezer bag. Seal, label, and freeze up to 8 months. To use, thaw the dough at room temperature for 2 to 3 hours or till thawed. (*Or,* thaw overnight in the refrigerator.)

Nutrition information per crust: 755 calories, 19 g protein, 132 g carbohydrate, 15 g fat (2 g saturated), 0 mg cholesterol, 272 mg sodium, 234 mg potassium.

Whole Wheat Pizza Crust
1¾ to 2¼ cups all-purpose flour
1 cup whole wheat flour

Prepare Pizza Crust as above, *except* use the 1¾ to 2¼ cups all-purpose flour and stir in the whole wheat flour after the beating step.

Nutrition information per crust: 727 calories, 21 g protein, 127 g carbohydrate, 16 g fat (2 g saturated), 0 mg cholesterol, 272 mg sodium, 396 mg potassium.

Tomatoey Pizza Sauce

If you're making only one pizza, place half the sauce in an airtight container and freeze up to 6 months. Thaw it overnight in the refrigerator before using. (Pictured on pages 68 and 69.)

¾ **cup chopped onion**
2 **cloves garlic, minced**
1 **tablespoon olive oil, margarine,**
  ***or* butter**

● In a medium saucepan cook onion and garlic in hot olive oil, margarine, or butter till onion is tender but not brown.

1 **14½-ounce can tomatoes, cut up**
1 **8-ounce can tomato sauce**
1 **bay leaf**
1 **teaspoon dried basil, crushed**
1 **teaspoon dried oregano, crushed**
½ **teaspoon sugar**
¼ **teaspoon pepper**

● Carefully stir in the *undrained* tomatoes, tomato sauce, bay leaf, basil, oregano, sugar, and pepper. Bring to boiling; reduce heat. Simmer, uncovered, for 25 to 30 minutes or to desired consistency, stirring occasionally. Discard bay leaf. Makes about 1½ cups sauce (enough for 2 pizzas).

Nutrition information per ¾ cup sauce: 167 calories, 5 g protein, 24 g carbohydrate, 8 g fat (1 g saturated), 0 mg cholesterol, 1,022 mg sodium, 1,014 mg potassium.

Creamy Parmesan Pizza Sauce

Team this sauce with a whole wheat crust and seafood topping for a rich and wonderful pizza. (Sauce pictured on pages 68 and 69.)

⅓ **cup finely chopped onion**
2 **cloves garlic, minced**
1 **tablespoon margarine *or* butter**
1 **tablespoon all-purpose flour**
⅛ **teaspoon white pepper**

● In a small saucepan cook the onion and garlic in hot margarine or butter till onion is tender but not brown. Stir in the flour and pepper.

1 **cup milk**
¼ **teaspoon instant chicken bouillon**
  granules
¼ **cup grated Parmesan *or* Romano**
  cheese
½ **teaspoon dried basil, crushed**

● Add the milk and chicken bouillon granules all at once. Cook and stir till slightly thickened and bubbly. Stir in the Parmesan or Romano cheese and basil. Makes about 1 cup sauce (enough for 1 pizza).

Nutrition information per 1 cup sauce: 375 calories, 19 g protein, 25 g carbohydrate, 23 g fat (9 g saturated), 38 mg cholesterol, 860 mg sodium, 544 mg potassium.

Pizza Toppings

To make a mouth-watering pizza, mix and match the toppings below. To start, prepare and prebake plain or whole wheat pizza crusts from page 66 or from tip box on page 71. Next, spread on Tomatoey Pizza Sauce or Creamy Parmesan Pizza Sauce from page 67, *or* use one 8-ounce can pizza sauce per pizza. Cover pizzas with your choice of toppings, totaling 3 to 4 cups per pizza, and finish baking.

Meats

Use ½ pound (about 1½ cups) of one of the following:
- cooked bulk Italian sausage
- cooked bulk pork sausage
- cooked ground turkey
- cooked ground beef
- cooked ground pork

Or, use 3 to 5 ounces (about 1 cup) of one of the following:
- cooked chopped chicken
- sliced pepperoni
- cut-up Canadian-style bacon
- cut-up fully cooked ham
- cut-up corned beef
- cut-up salami

Seafood

Use ½ pound (about 1½ cups) of one of the following:
- cooked scallops
- cooked peeled and deveined shrimp

Or, use one 6½-ounce can of one of the following:
- chunk white tuna, drained
- skinless, boneless salmon, drained
- crabmeat, drained, flaked, and cartilage removed

Vegetables

Use 1 cup of one of the following (steam vegetables about 2 minutes and drain before adding to the pizza):
- sliced zucchini
- sliced yellow summer squash
- broccoli flowerets

Or, use half of a 9-ounce package (about 1 cup) of one of the following (thaw and drain before adding to the pizza):
- frozen artichoke hearts
- frozen chopped spinach

Vegetables

In addition, use one of the following:
- 1 cup sliced fresh mushrooms
- 2 medium ripe fresh tomatoes, sliced (about 1 cup)
- 1 medium onion or leek, thinly sliced (about ½ cup)
- 1 medium green, sweet red, or yellow pepper, thinly sliced (about ¾ cup)

Other Additions

Use one of the following:
- one 2-ounce can anchovy fillets, drained
- one 6½-ounce can minced clams, drained
- 6 slices bacon, cooked and crumbled
- one 2½-ounce can sliced, pitted ripe olives, drained

Cheeses

Use 1 to 2 cups of one or more of the following:
- shredded mozzarella
- shredded provolone
- shredded cheddar

In addition, use ¼ cup of one of the following:
- grated Parmesan
- grated Romano
- grated asiago

69

Pizza Rustica

2 slightly beaten eggs
1¼ cups ricotta cheese
½ cup shredded mozzarella cheese (2 ounces)
½ cup shredded provolone cheese (2 ounces)
2 tablespoons grated Parmesan *or* Romano cheese
¼ teaspoon ground cinnamon
4 ounces thinly sliced prosciutto *or* fully cooked ham, cut into strips
4 ounces mortadella *or* salami, chopped

● For filling, in a medium mixing bowl stir together the eggs, ricotta cheese, mozzarella cheese, provolone cheese, Parmesan or Romano cheese, and cinnamon. Add prosciutto or ham and mortadella or salami; stir till mixed. Set aside.

2 cups all-purpose flour
1 tablespoon sugar
½ teaspoon salt
⅔ cup shortening *or* lard
6 to 7 tablespoons cold water

● In a mixing bowl combine flour, sugar, and salt. Cut in shortening till pieces are the size of small peas. Sprinkle *1 tablespoon* of the water over part of mixture; gently toss with a fork. Push to the side of the bowl. Repeat till all is moistened. Divide in half; shape into balls.

Milk

● On a lightly floured surface, flatten one ball of dough with hands. Roll dough from center to edges, forming a circle about 12 inches in diameter. Wrap pastry around rolling pin. Unroll onto a 9-inch pie plate. Ease pastry into pie plate. Trim pastry to edge of the plate. Add the filling. For top crust, roll out remaining dough. Cut slits to allow steam to escape. Place top crust on filling. Trim top crust ½ inch beyond edge of plate. Fold top crust under bottom crust; flute edge. Lightly brush with milk. Bake in a 375° oven for 50 to 55 minutes or till crust is golden. Let stand for 5 minutes before serving. Makes 6 to 8 main-dish servings or 12 appetizer-size servings.

Nutrition information per serving: 631 calories, 26 g protein, 37 g carbohydrate, 42 g fat (16 g saturated), 131 mg cholesterol, 887 mg sodium, 208 mg potassium.

Spinach-Filled Pizza Rustica
1 10-ounce package frozen chopped spinach

Prepare Pizza Rustica as directed above, *except* omit the mortadella or salami. Cook the spinach according to package directions. Drain well. Pat with paper towels to remove moisture. Stir spinach into filling.

Nutrition information per serving: 585 calories, 24 g protein, 39 g carbohydrate, 37 g fat (14 g saturated), 121 mg cholesterol, 692 mg sodium, 318 mg potassium.

Sausage and Mushroom Calzones

Serve these individual stuffed pizzas the next time you have a few friends over.

1 **16-ounce loaf frozen bread dough, thawed**

● Divide loaf into 6 equal pieces. Shape into balls. On a lightly floured surface, roll each ball of dough into a circle about 7 inches in diameter. Cover to prevent from drying out.

¾ **pound bulk Italian sausage**
1 **cup sliced fresh mushrooms**
⅓ **cup chopped onion**
⅓ **cup chopped green pepper (optional)**
½ **recipe Tomatoey Pizza Sauce (see recipe, page 67)** *or* **one 8-ounce can pizza sauce**
1½ **cups shredded mozzarella cheese (6 ounces)**

● In a large skillet cook sausage, mushrooms, onion, and, if desired, green pepper till sausage is brown and onion is tender. Drain fat. Pat with paper towels to remove additional fat. Stir in pizza sauce. Spoon meat mixture on *half* of *each* circle to within ½ inch of the edge. Sprinkle about ¼ *cup* mozzarella cheese over meat mixture on *each* circle.

Milk
1 **tablespoon grated Parmesan cheese**

● Moisten edges of dough with water. Fold dough in half over filling. Seal by pressing with tines of a fork. Prick tops. Lightly brush tops with milk. Sprinkle with Parmesan cheese. Place calzones 2 to 3 inches apart on a greased large baking sheet. Bake in a 375° oven for 20 to 25 mintues or till crust is lightly browned. Makes 6 main-dish servings.

Nutrition information per serving: 420 calories, 24 g protein, 40 g carbohydrate, 19 g fat (7 g saturated), 50 mg cholesterol, 1,079 mg sodium, 384 mg potassium.

Pizza Crust In a Flash

For a quick substitute to the Pizza Crust recipe on page 66, make the dough from one of the convenience products listed at right. Unless specified otherwise, just shape, top, and bake according to the instructions for the homemade crust.

● One 16-ounce loaf frozen bread dough (white or wheat), thawed and halved.
● Two 10-ounce packages refrigerated pizza dough. If making thick crusts, omit the rising time.
● One 16-ounce package hot roll mix. Prepare according to package directions for pizza dough.
● Packaged biscuit mix. Prepare according to package directions for pizza crust, making enough for two crusts.

Zesty Italian Peasant Pizza

Look for the Italian bread shell, a round, flat, prebaked bread, in refrigerator cases in large supermarkets and specialty food shops.

1 16-ounce Italian bread shell

● Place Italian bread shell on a lightly greased baking sheet.

1 to 2 tablespoons olive oil *or* cooking oil
1 clove garlic, minced
⅛ teaspoon pepper
1 medium ripe fresh tomato, peeled, seeded, and chopped (¾ cup)
¼ cup crumbled Gorgonzola *or* blue cheese (1 ounce)
1 tablespoon snipped fresh rosemary, oregano, *or* basil, *or* 1 teaspoon dried rosemary, oregano, *or* basil, crushed.

● In a small mixing bowl stir together the olive oil or cooking oil, garlic, and pepper. Brush generously over the bread shell. Sprinkle the tomato, Gorgonzola or blue cheese, and rosemary, oregano, or basil over the bread shell.

Fresh rosemary, oregano, *or* basil sprigs (optional)

● Bake in a 400° oven about 10 minutes or till warm and cheese melts. If desired, garnish with fresh rosemary, oregano, or basil. Cut into wedges. Makes 4 to 6 side-dish servings or 8 appetizer-size servings.

Nutrition information per serving: 379 calories, 12 g protein, 66 g carbohydrate, 7 g fat (2 g saturated), 6 mg cholesterol, 796 mg sodium, 160 mg potassium.

Red Onion and Tomato Peasant Pizza
½ of a medium red onion, thinly sliced and separated into rings
2 tablespoons grated Parmesan cheese

Prepare Zesty Italian Peasant Pizza as directed above, *except* layer the red onion with the tomato over the bread shell. Substitute the Parmesan cheese for the Gorgonzola or blue cheese.

Nutrition information per serving: 371 calories, 12 g protein, 67 g carbohydrate, 5 g fat (1 g saturated), 2 mg cholesterol, 716 mg sodium, 190 mg potassium.

Mozzarella Cheese Sandwiches

For a boost of flavor, dip these crusty cheese sandwich triangles in your favorite pizza sauce.

6 ounces sliced mozzarella cheese
8 slices firm-texture white bread

● Place mozzarella cheese slices on half of the bread slices. Trim cheese to fit. Top with remaining bread slices.

2 beaten eggs
⅓ cup milk
¾ cup fine dry Italian seasoned bread crumbs

● In a pie plate or shallow bowl combine the eggs and milk. Dip both sides of the cheese sandwiches in the egg mixture, then in the bread crumbs.

2 tablespoons margarine *or* butter

● In a large skillet cook *2* of the sandwiches in *1 tablespoon* of the hot margarine or butter over medium to medium-low heat for 2 to 3 minutes on each side or till crisp. Keep warm in a 300° oven. Carefully wipe out skillet. Repeat with the remaining sandwiches and margarine or butter. Cut each sandwich into 4 triangles. Makes 4 main-dish servings.

Nutrition information per serving: 456 calories, 22 g protein, 49 g carbohydrate, 19 g fat (8 g saturated), 133 mg cholesterol, 784 mg sodium, 176 mg potassium.

Casual Party

An old Italian tradition that is still practiced in that country is to feature the main meal at noon. A light meal or snack (*spuntino*) is then served in the evening as family and friends gather. To Americans, the type of foods served would be considered finger foods.

In this menu, finger foods such as Cheesy Hot Sandwich Loaf and its accompaniments are just right for casual entertaining. Serving the meal on paper plates and without any silverware makes the cleanup easy and the entertaining hassle-free!

Menu

Cheesy Hot Sandwich Loaf

(see recipe, page 74)

Cut-up fresh vegetables

Assorted fruits and cheeses

Amaretti Cookies

(see recipe, page 124)

or purchased Amaretti cookies

Cheesy Hot Sandwich Loaf

The freshly baked bread holds three yummy cheeses.

1 16-ounce package hot-roll mix

● Prepare hot-roll mix through the kneading step according to basic recipe on package directions. Cover and let rest 5 minutes.

4 ounces thinly sliced fully cooked ham, cut into strips
4 ounces thinly sliced pepperoni, cut into strips
1 cup ricotta cheese
1 cup shredded mozzarella *or* provolone cheese (4 ounces)
1 cup shredded fontina *or* fontinella cheese (4 ounces)
⅓ cup thinly sliced green onion
¼ teaspoon pepper

● For filling, in a large mixing bowl stir together the ham, pepperoni, ricotta cheese, mozzarella or provolone cheese, fontina or fontinella cheese, green onion, and pepper. Set aside.

● Grease a large baking sheet. Set aside. On a lightly floured surface, roll the dough into a 12x9-inch rectangle. Spread the filling lengthwise down the center of the rectangle in a 4-inch-wide strip. Fold long sides of dough over filling. Moisten edges with water. Pinch to seal. Place loaf seam side down on the prepared baking sheet. With a very sharp knife, cut 1½-inch slits in the top for steam to escape. Cover and let rise for 10 minutes.

Milk
Sesame seed (optional)

● Lightly brush loaf with milk. If desired, sprinkle with sesame seed. Bake in a 375° oven about 20 minutes or till golden. Let stand for 5 minutes. Using a serrated knife, slice into serving-size pieces. Makes 8 main-dish servings or 16 appetizer-size servings.

Nutrition information per serving: 440 calories, 23 g protein, 44 g carbohydrate, 19 g fat (9 g saturated), 53 mg cholesterol, 961 mg sodium, 244 mg potassium.

**Cheesy Hot
Sandwich Loaf**

Italian Sausage Sandwich

1 16-ounce loaf unsliced Italian *or* French bread (about 16x4 inches)	● Split bread loaf in half horizontally. Hollow out bottom half of the loaf. Set aside.
½ pound bulk Italian sausage **½ pound ground beef** **¾ cup chopped onion** **½ cup chopped green pepper** **1 cup Tomatoey Pizza Sauce (see recipe, page 67) *or* 1 cup purchased pizza sauce** **¼ cup grated Parmesan cheese** **1 4-ounce can mushroom stems and pieces, drained** **½ teaspoon fennel seed, crushed (optional)**	● In a large skillet cook sausage, ground beef, onion, and green pepper till no pink remains in the meat. Drain fat well. Stir in pizza sauce, Parmesan cheese, mushrooms, and, if desired, fennel seed. Heat through.
3 ounces sliced mozzarella cheese **3 ounces sliced cheddar cheese**	● Spoon meat mixture into the bottom half of the loaf. Arrange mozzarella cheese and cheddar cheese over top of meat mixture. Cover with loaf top. Place sandwich in a shallow baking pan or on a baking sheet. Cover tightly with foil and heat in a 375° oven about 15 minutes or till cheese melts and sandwich is hot. Using a serrated knife, slice into 6 portions. Makes 6 main-dish servings.

Nutrition information per serving: 536 calories, 30 g protein, 52 g carbohydrate, 23 g fat (10 g saturated), 72 mg cholesterol, 1,251 mg sodium, 552 mg potassium.

Italy's Specialty Cheeses

Cooks in Italy use numerous varieties of cheese for snacking and cooking. The cheeses are produced on small farms and sold at local markets. In America, special varieties of Italian cheese are available at Italian specialty stores or deli counters in supermarkets.

● *Asiago* is a cow's-milk cheese that is nutty, rich, and somewhat piquant when young. As it ages, it gets harder and sharper. Asiago is a wonderful cheese to shred and use interchangeably with Parmesan to sprinkle over pasta.

● *Bel Paese* is a cow's-milk cheese with a creamy texture and a mild flavor. Bel Paese is great to use for snacking or for cooking.

● *Fontina* is a cow's-milk cheese that develops its nutty, creamy, and smooth characteristics through three months of ripening. Fontina is a superb cheese not only for snacking but also for cooking.

● *Gorgonzola* is a blue-veined variety of cow's-milk cheese that is smooth and easy to spread. Its robust flavor and creamy texture make it a great cheese for snacking and for cooking.

Italian-Style Poor-Boy Sandwich

4 **Mini Italian Loaves (see recipe, page 84)** *or* **4 French-style rolls**
6 **ounces sliced mozzarella** *or* **provolone cheese**
6 **ounces thinly sliced salami**
6 **ounces thinly sliced cappicola** *or* **fully cooked ham**
2 **medium ripe fresh tomatoes, thinly sliced**
1⅓ **cups shredded lettuce**
1 **small onion, thinly sliced and separated into rings**
  Italian Vinaigrette (see recipe, page 105)

● Split bread loaves or rolls in half horizontally. On the cut side of the bottoms, layer mozzarella or provolone cheese, salami, cappicola or fully cooked ham, tomatoes, lettuce, and onion. Drizzle Italian Vinaigrette over the layers. Add tops of loaves or rolls. Makes 4 main-dish servings.

Nutrition information per serving: 868 calories, 45 g protein, 96 g carbohydrate, 34 g fat (12 g saturated), 81 mg cholesterol, 2,177 mg sodium, 670 mg potassium.

Pepper and Provolone Sandwich

Savor the flavor of onions and peppers embedded in fresh bread and smothered with cheese.

2 **medium onions, thinly sliced and separated into rings**
1 **medium green pepper, cut into thin strips**
1 **medium sweet red pepper, cut into thin strips**
1 **medium sweet yellow pepper, cut into thin strips**
2 **cloves garlic, minced**
½ **teaspoon dried basil, crushed**
¼ **teaspoon dried oregano, crushed**
2 **tablespoons olive oil** *or* **cooking oil**
1 **tablespoon margarine** *or* **butter**

● In a 12-inch skillet cook onions, green pepper, red pepper, yellow pepper, garlic, basil, and oregano in hot olive oil or cooking oil and margarine or butter for 8 to 10 minutes or till vegetables are tender, stirring occasionally.

1 **16-ounce loaf unsliced Italian** *or* **French bread (about 16x4 inches)**
10 **ounces sliced provolone** *or* **mozzarella cheese**

● Meanwhile, split bread loaf in half horizontally, *not* slicing all the way through. Place opened loaf on a large baking sheet. Place *half* the provolone or mozzarella slices on the bottom half of the loaf. Place cooked vegetable mixture over cheese. Top with remaining cheese. Broil 4 to 5 inches from the heat about 3 minutes or till cheese is bubbly. Remove from oven. Fold bread over cheese. Using a serrated knife, slice into 4 portions. Makes 4 main-dish servings.

Nutrition information per serving: 675 calories, 29 g protein, 71 g carbohydrate, 30 g fat (14 g saturated), 50 mg cholesterol, 1,320 mg sodium, 346 mg potassium.

SOUPS & BREADS

Italian cooks are known for their potpourri of piping hot

soups. They've created light broth-based soups

to serve as accompaniments to meals as well as hearty tomato-based

main-dish soups. To make any meal tummy-warming,

include a soup and a golden-crusted bread from this chapter.

Chicken and Tortellini Soup

Frozen tortellini works as well as dry packaged. Just check doneness 1 to 2 minutes sooner.

2½ **cups water**
1 **10¾-ounce can condensed cream of chicken soup**
1 **medium carrot, chopped (½ cup)**
1 **small onion, chopped (⅓ cup)**
1 **teaspoon dried Italian seasoning, crushed**
⅛ **teaspoon pepper**

● In a large saucepan stir together the water, cream of chicken soup, carrot, onion, Italian seasoning, and pepper. Heat to boiling; reduce heat. Cover and simmer for 20 minutes.

1 **cup packaged cheese tortellini**
1 **cup fresh *or* frozen chopped broccoli**
1½ **cups chopped cooked chicken (8 ounces)**

● Stir in the tortellini and broccoli. Cover and simmer about 15 minutes more or till tortellini is tender. Stir in chicken and heat through.

¼ **cup finely shredded *or* grated Parmesan cheese**
1 **tablespoon snipped parsley**

● To serve, ladle soup into bowls. Sprinkle with Parmesan cheese and parsley. Makes 4 main-dish servings.

Nutrition information per serving: 312 calories, 28 g protein, 27 g carbohydrate, 10 g fat (3 g saturated), 76 mg cholesterol, 896 mg sodium, 393 mg potassium.

Roman Egg Drop Soup

It's the cheese that makes this soup distinctively Italian.

2 **14½-ounce cans chicken broth**
½ **of a 10-ounce package frozen chopped spinach**

● In a large saucepan heat broth to boiling. Add the spinach and return to boiling; reduce heat. Cover and simmer for 3 to 5 minutes or till spinach is tender.

1 **beaten egg**
2 **tablespoons grated Parmesan *or* Romano cheese**

● Meanwhile, stir together the egg and cheese. Slowly pour egg mixture into simmering broth. Stir gently, forming tiny shreds of egg. Serve immediately. Makes 4 side-dish servings.

Nutrition information per serving: 71 calories, 8 g protein, 3 g carbohydrate, 3 g fat (1 g saturated), 56 mg cholesterol, 747 mg sodium, 285 mg potassium.

**Parmesan and
Onion Flat Bread**
(see recipe, page 88)

Minestrone

Minestrone

The countless versions of this soup all have one thing in common—they're chock-full of garden vegetable goodness.

2 medium onions, chopped (1 cup), *or*
   2 medium leeks, sliced
1 medium carrot, chopped (½ cup)
1 stalk celery, sliced (½ cup)
1 clove garlic, minced
2 tablespoons olive oil *or* **cooking oil**

● In a large Dutch oven or kettle, cook onions or leeks, carrot, celery, and garlic in hot olive oil or cooking oil till onion is tender but not brown.

2 14½-ounce cans chicken *or* **beef**
   broth
1 16-ounce can tomatoes, cut up
1 cup shredded cabbage
¾ cup tomato juice
1 teaspoon dried basil, crushed

● Stir in the chicken or beef broth, *undrained* tomatoes, cabbage, tomato juice, and basil. Bring to boiling; reduce heat. Cover and simmer for 20 minutes.

1 15-ounce can cannellini *or* **great**
   northern beans, rinsed and drained
1 medium zucchini, sliced ¼ inch thick
   (1 cup)
½ of a 9-ounce package frozen Italian-
   style green beans
2 ounces packaged spaghetti *or*
   linguine, broken (about ½ cup)
2 ounces prosciutto *or* **fully cooked**
   ham, diced
¼ cup finely shredded Parmesan cheese
   or **¼ cup Pesto (see recipe,**
   page 16)

● Stir in the cannellini or great northern beans, zucchini, green beans, spaghetti or linguine, and prosciutto or ham. Return to boiling; reduce heat. Cover and simmer for 10 to 15 minutes more or till vegetables and pasta are tender. To serve, ladle soup into bowls and top with Parmesan cheese or Pesto. Makes 4 main-dish or 8 side-dish servings.

Nutrition information per serving: 372 calories, 23 g protein, 48 g carbohydrate, 11 g fat (3 g saturated), 12 mg cholesterol, 1,307 mg sodium, 1,307 mg potassium.

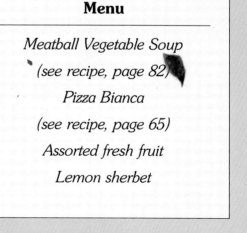

Soup Supper

Making soup is an ancient way of cooking and one that is most cherished by Italian cooks. Meatball Vegetable Soup exemplifies the tantalizing flavor that is developed through the blending and cooking of fresh ingredients.

   Hearty soups that are rich in vegetables and meat are perfect to serve with bread, or in this case a cheesy no-sauce pizza, for a nutritious meal.

Menu

Meatball Vegetable Soup

(see recipe, page 82)

Pizza Bianca

(see recipe, page 65)

Assorted fresh fruit

Lemon sherbet

Meatball Vegetable Soup

1 beaten egg
½ cup soft bread crumbs (⅔ slice)
3 tablespoons grated Romano *or*
   Parmesan cheese
1 tablespoon snipped parsley
1 tablespoon finely chopped onion
½ pound ground beef

● In a medium mixing bowl stir together the egg, bread crumbs, Romano or Parmesan cheese, parsley, and onion. Add the ground beef and mix well. Shape meat mixture into 36 equal-size balls. In a large skillet cook the meatballs about 8 minutes or till no pink remains. Drain fat. Set aside.

3 cups beef broth
1 16-ounce can tomatoes, cut up, *or*
   3 ripe fresh tomatoes, peeled and
   chopped (2 cups)
2 medium carrots, thinly sliced (1 cup)
¾ cup chopped onion
½ of a 6-ounce can (⅓ cup), tomato
   paste
1 teaspoon dried basil, crushed
⅛ teaspoon pepper
3 cups torn fresh spinach

● In a large saucepan stir together the beef broth, *undrained* tomatoes, carrots, onion, tomato paste, basil, and pepper. Bring to boiling; reduce heat. Cover and simmer about 20 minutes or till carrots are nearly tender. Add the meatballs and heat through.
   Stir in spinach. Cook 1 to 2 minutes or just till spinach is wilted. Makes 4 main-dish or 6 side-dish servings.

Nutrition information per serving: 259 calories, 20 g protein, 20 g carbohydrate, 12 g fat (5 g saturated), 96 mg cholesterol, 972 mg sodium, 1,104 mg potassium.

Beef and Barley Soup

Barley is a common soup ingredient in many regions of Italy.

2 pounds beef short ribs *or* 1 pound
   beef chuck steak
1 large onion, thinly sliced and
   separated into rings
2 cloves garlic, minced
2 tablespoons cooking oil

● Trim fat from ribs or steak. If using steak, cut into ¾-inch cubes. In a Dutch oven cook ribs or steak cubes, onion, and garlic in hot cooking oil till meat is brown and onion is tender, turning and stirring as needed. Drain fat.

7 cups water
3 medium carrots, chopped (1½ cups)
2 stalks celery, sliced (1 cup)
2 tablespoons snipped parsley
2 bay leaves
1 tablespoon instant beef bouillon
   granules
½ teaspoon dried thyme, crushed
½ teaspoon dried rosemary, crushed
¼ teaspoon pepper
⅓ cup pearl barley

● Stir in water, carrots, celery, parsley, bay leaves, beef bouillon granules, thyme, rosemary, and pepper. Bring to boiling; reduce heat. Cover and simmer 45 minutes. Stir in barley. Cover and simmer 50 to 60 minutes more or till meat is tender. Skim fat from soup.
   If using ribs, remove from soup. When cool enough to handle, remove meat from bones. Discard bones. Cut the meat into bite-size pieces. Return meat to soup and heat through. Discard the bay leaves. Makes 4 main-dish or 8 side-dish servings.

Nutrition information per serving: 392 calories, 29 g protein, 22 g carbohydrate, 20 g fat (6 g saturated), 90 mg cholesterol, 805 mg sodium, 562 mg potassium.

Italian-Style Fish Soup

Four kinds of fish and seafood cook in a tomato-flavored broth.

½ **pound fresh *or* frozen haddock, bass, sole, or other fish fillets**
8 **ounces fresh *or* frozen peeled shrimp**
4 **to 8 clams in shells**

● Thaw fish and shrimp, if frozen. Cut fish into 1-inch pieces. Set fish pieces and shrimp aside. Wash and scrub clams. Cover clams with salted water, using 3 tablespoons *salt* to 8 cups *water*. Soak for 15 minutes, then rinse. Discard water. Repeat soaking and rinsing clams twice. Drain and set aside.

1 **medium onion, chopped (½ cup)**
1 **medium green pepper, chopped (½ cup)**
1 **clove garlic, minced**
1 **tablespoon olive oil *or* cooking oil**
1 **14½-ounce can chicken broth**
1 **10½-ounce can tomato puree**
2 **medium ripe fresh tomatoes, peeled, seeded, and cut up**
⅓ **cup dry red wine**
1 **bay leaf**
½ **teaspoon dried basil, crushed**
¼ **teaspoon dried oregano, crushed**
⅛ **teaspoon pepper**

● In a large saucepan or Dutch oven, cook the onion, green pepper, and garlic in hot olive oil or cooking oil till vegetables are tender but not brown. Carefully stir in the chicken broth, tomato puree, tomatoes, wine, bay leaf, basil, oregano, and pepper. Bring to boiling; reduce heat. Cover and simmer for 20 minutes, stirring occasionally.

1 **5-ounce can lobster, drained, broken into pieces, and cartilage removed**
2 **tablespoons snipped parsley**

● Stir the fish, shrimp, clams, and lobster into the soup. Return to boiling; reduce heat. Cover and simmer for 5 to 10 minutes more or till clams open and fish flakes easily with a fork. Discard the bay leaf and any clams that did not open. Stir in the parsley. Makes 4 main-dish servings.

Nutrition information per serving: 238 calories, 31 g protein, 14 g carbohydrate, 5 g fat (1 g saturated), 138 mg cholesterol, 594 mg sodium, 996 mg potassium.

Italian Bread

Oh, so good. (Breadsticks pictured on page 7 and Mini Italian Loaves pictured on page 50.)

5½ **to 6 cups all-purpose flour**
2 **packages active dry yeast**
1½ **teaspoons salt**
2 **cups warm water (120° to 130°)**

● In a large mixing bowl combine *2 cups* of the flour, yeast, and salt. Add water. Beat with an electric mixer on low speed 30 seconds, scraping bowl. Beat on high speed 3 minutes. Stir in as much remaining flour as you can. On a floured surface, knead in enough remaining flour to make a stiff dough that is smooth and elastic (8 to 10 minutes). Shape into a ball. Place in a greased bowl; turn once. Cover; let rise in warm place till double (1 to 1½ hours).

Cornmeal
1 **slightly beaten egg white**
1 **tablespoon water**
¼ **teaspoon dried rosemary *or* basil, crushed, *or* ⅛ teaspoon onion powder *or* garlic powder (optional)**

● Punch down. Divide in half. Cover; let rest 10 minutes. Grease 2 baking sheets and sprinkle with cornmeal. Roll each half into a 15x12-inch rectangle. Roll up from long side; seal well. Taper ends. Place, seam side down, on prepared baking sheets. Brush with a mixture of egg white; water; and if desired, an herb or onion powder. Cover; let rise till *nearly* double (about 45 minutes). Make 5 or 6 diagonal cuts ¼ inch deep across tops. Bake in a 375° oven 20 minutes. Brush again with egg white mixture. Bake 20 to 25 minutes or till golden. Cool. Makes 2 loaves (30 servings).

Mini Italian Loaves

Prepare Italian Bread as above, *except* divide each half of dough into thirds. Cover; let rest 10 minutes. Shape each into an 8-inch loaf; taper ends. Place on prepared baking sheets. Brush with egg white mixture; let rise as above. Make 2 or 3 diagonal shallow cuts across tops. Bake in a 375° oven 15 minutes. Brush with egg white mixture. Bake about 10 minutes or till golden. Cool. Makes 6 loaves (30 servings).

Breadsticks

Prepare Italian Bread as above, *except* divide each half of dough into 15 pieces. Roll each into an 8-inch rope. Place on prepared baking sheets. Cover and let rise till *nearly* double (about 30 minutes). Brush with the egg white mixture. Bake in a 375° oven for 10 minutes. Brush again with egg white mixture. Reduce temperature to 300° and bake for 20 to 25 minutes or till golden. Cool. Makes 30.

Nutrition information per serving or breadstick: 85 calories, 3 g protein, 18 g carbohydrate, 0 g fat (0 g saturated), 0 mg cholesterol, 109 mg sodium, 33 mg potassium.

Sunflower Nut Italian Loaves

The crisp crust and chewy interior resemble that of regular Italian bread.

1 cup boiling water
½ cup cracked wheat

● Pour the boiling water over cracked wheat. Let stand about 10 minutes or till most of the liquid is absorbed. Set aside.

4¼ to 4¾ cups all-purpose flour
1 package active dry yeast
1½ teaspoons salt
1 cup warm water (120° to 130°)
1 tablespoon cooking oil
¼ cup sunflower nuts

● Meanwhile, in a large mixing bowl stir together *1½ cups* of the flour, the yeast, and salt. Add the warm water and cooking oil. Beat with an electric mixer on low speed for 30 seconds, scraping bowl. Beat on high speed for 3 minutes. Using a spoon, stir in the cracked wheat and sunflower nuts. Stir in as much of the remaining flour as you can.

● Turn dough out onto a lightly floured surface. Knead in enough of the remaining flour to make a stiff dough that is smooth and elastic (8 to 10 minutes total). Shape into a ball. Place in a lightly greased bowl; turn once to grease surface. Cover and let rise in a warm place till double (1 to 1¼ hours).

Cornmeal
1 slightly beaten egg white
1 tablespoon water

● Punch dough down. Turn out onto a lightly floured surface. Divide in half. Cover and let rest for 10 minutes. Grease 2 baking sheets and sprinkle with cornmeal. Roll each half into a 15x11-inch rectangle. Roll up tightly from long side; seal well. Taper ends. Place, seam side down, on prepared baking sheet. Brush with a mixture of egg white and water. Cover and let rise till *nearly* double (about 45 minutes).

Using a very sharp knife, make 3 or 4 diagonal cuts about ¼ inch deep across the top of each loaf. Bake in a 375° oven for 20 minutes. Brush again with egg white mixture. Bake 10 to 15 minutes more or till bread sounds hollow when tapped. Cool on wire racks. Makes 2 loaves (30 servings).

Nutrition information per serving: 82 calories, 2 g protein, 15 g carbohydrate, 1 g fat (0 g saturated), 0 mg cholesterol, 108 sodium, 39 potassium.

Bread Fix-Ups

Add some Italian flair to any meal by dressing up the bread you serve. Try one of these quick and easy ideas.

Idea 1: Unroll 1 package (8) *refrigerated breadsticks* without separating. Sprinkle ¼ cup finely chopped *onion* and 1 teaspoon crushed dried *Italian seasoning* over dough. Roll up, starting from a short side. Slice where perforated. Place coils in a greased 9x1½-inch round baking pan. Bake in a 375° oven for 15 to 17 minutes or till golden. Remove from pan. Makes 8 rolls.

Nutrition information per roll: 102 calories, 3 g protein, 18 g carbohydrate, 2 g fat (0 g saturated), 0 mg cholesterol, 230 mg sodium, 32 mg potassium.

Idea 2: Separate a package of *refrigerated breadsticks*. Un-coil and cut each breadstick in half. Twist dough. In a small bowl combine some grated *Parmesan or Romano cheese* and a few dashes ground *red pepper*. Brush dough with beaten *egg,* then sprinkle with cheese mixture. Bake according to package directions.

Idea 3: Separate a package of *refrigerated biscuits*. Pat or roll each to a 3-inch circle. Place on an ungreased baking sheet. Lightly brush circles with *olive oil.* Place a thin *tomato slice* in the center of each circle. Sprinkle lightly with crushed dried *oregano* and finely shredded or grated *Parmesan cheese*. Bake in a 400° oven for 8 to 10 minutes or till golden.

Idea 4: Cut one 16-ounce loaf *Italian bread* (about 14 inches long) in half horizontally. In a small mixing bowl stir together ⅔ cup *mayonnaise or salad dressing*, ½ cup grated *Parmesan or Romano cheese*, and 1 tablespoon *Pesto* (see recipe, page 16) or purchased *pesto*. Spread over cut sides of bread. Place bread, pesto side up, on the unheated rack of a broiler pan. Broil 4 to 5 inches from heat for 2 to 3 minutes or till bubbly. Sprinkle lightly with crushed *red pepper*. Cut diagonally into 2-inch slices. Makes 14 slices.

Nutrition information per slice: 184 calories, 4 g protein, 19 g carbohydrate, 10 g fat (2 g saturated), 9 mg cholesterol, 309 mg sodium, 37 mg potassium.

Idea 5: Brush 1 side of ¾-inch-thick slices of *Italian bread* with melted *margarine or butter*. Sprinkle with a little crushed, dried *basil* and some grated *Parmesan cheese*. Place bread slices, cheese side up, on the unheated rack of a broiler pan. Broil 4 to 5 inches from heat for 2 to 3 minutes or till cheese is golden.

Idea 6: Brush 1 side of ¾-inch-thick slices of *Italian bread* with some melted *margarine or butter*. Sprinkle lightly with *garlic powder*. Then generously sprinkle with shredded *mozzarella cheese*. Place bread slices, cheese side up, on the unheated rack of a broiler pan. Broil 4 to 5 inches from heat for 2 to 3 minutes or till cheese is golden and bubbly.

Idea 7: Separate a package of *refrigerated breadsticks*. Uncoil and cut each breadstick in half. Place a thin strip of thinly sliced *prosciutto or fully cooked ham* lengthwise on each breadstick half, and twist. Bake according to package directions.

87

Gorgonzola and Onion Flat Bread

To prevent over-rising, place part of the dough portions in the refrigerator while baking the others. (Parmesan and Onion Flat Bread is pictured on page 80.)

2¼ to 2¾ cups all-purpose flour
 1 package active dry yeast
 1 teaspoon salt
 1 cup warm water (120° to 130°)
 3 tablespoons olive oil *or* cooking oil
 ½ cup whole wheat *or* rye flour

● In a large mixing bowl stir together *1 cup* of the all-purpose flour, the yeast, and salt. Add the warm water and oil. Beat with an electric mixer on low speed for 30 seconds, scraping bowl. Beat on high speed for 3 minutes. Using a spoon, stir in the whole wheat or rye flour and as much of the remaining all-purpose flour as you can. Turn out onto a lightly floured surface. Knead in enough of the remaining flour to make a moderately stiff dough that is smooth and elastic (6 to 8 minutes total). Shape into a ball. Place in a greased bowl; turn once to grease surface. Cover and let rise in a warm place till double (about 1 hour).

 3 medium onions, thinly sliced and
 separated into rings
 3 tablespoons olive oil or cooking oil

● Punch dough down. Turn out onto a lightly floured surface. Divide dough into sixths and shape into balls. Cover and let rest for 10 minutes. Meanwhile, cook the onions in hot olive oil or cooking oil till very tender but not brown. Set cooked onions aside.

 ¾ cup finely chopped walnuts
 1 cup crumbled Gorgonzola or blue
 cheese (4 ounces)

● Cover and refrigerate 4 portions of dough. Roll remaining 2 portions into 8-inch rounds. Top *each* round with *one-sixth* of the walnuts and the onion mixture. Transfer rounds to a greased baking sheet. Cover; let rise in a warm place for 15 minutes. Bake in a 450° oven for 8 minutes. Sprinkle *one-sixth* of the Gorgonzola or blue cheese over *each* round. Bake for 4 to 6 minutes more or till crisp and golden. Repeat rolling, topping, rising, and baking of remaining portions of dough. To store the flat bread, wrap in plastic wrap and refrigerate up to 3 days. Makes 6 rounds (12 servings).

Nutrition information per serving: 253 calories, 7 g protein, 24 g carbohydrate, 15 g fat (3 g saturated), 8 mg cholesterol, 350 mg sodium, 121 mg potassium.

Parmesan and Onion Flat Bread
 ½ teaspoon dried thyme, crushed
 ¾ cup finely shredded Parmesan cheese

Prepare Gorgonzola and Onion Flat Bread as above, *except* add the thyme to onions while cooking. Omit walnuts and substitute Parmesan cheese for Gorgonzola or blue cheese.

Nutrition information per serving: 190 calories, 5 g protein, 23 g carbohydrate, 9 g fat (2 g saturated), 4 mg cholesterol, 267 mg sodium, 80 mg potassium.

Onion-Herb Focaccia

1 **16-ounce package hot-roll mix *or* one 16-ounce loaf frozen bread dough, thawed**

● Grease 3 baking sheets or pizza pans. Set aside. If using hot-roll mix, prepare according to package directions through kneading and resting steps. Divide dough into thirds; shape into balls. Roll each dough ball into a 10-inch round. Place on prepared baking sheets. Cover.

1 **cup chopped onion**
1 **tablespoon snipped fresh rosemary *or* basil *or* 1 teaspoon dried rosemary *or* basil, crushed**
¼ **cup olive oil *or* cooking oil**

● In a medium skillet cook onion and herb in hot oil till onion is tender but not brown. Press slight indentations in dough rounds with fingertips. Evenly top with cooked onion mixture. Cover; let rise in warm place till *nearly* double (30 to 40 minutes). Bake in a 375° oven for 12 to 15 minutes or till golden. Cool. To store, wrap in plastic wrap and refrigerate up to 3 days. Makes 3 rounds (12 servings).

Nutrition information per serving: 179 calories, 4 g protein, 29 g carbohydrate, 5 g fat (1 g saturated), 0 mg cholesterol, 261 mg sodium, 75 mg potassium.

Panettone

3 to 3½ **cups all-purpose flour**
1 **package active dry yeast**
½ **cup milk**
¼ **cup honey**
¼ **cup margarine *or* butter**
½ **teaspoon salt**
2 **eggs**
¼ **cup light raisins**
¼ **cup dried currants**
¼ **cup chopped candied citron**
1½ **teaspoons crushed anise seed**

● Combine *1 cup* of the flour and yeast. Heat and stir milk, honey, margarine, and salt just till warm (120° to 130°) and margarine almost melts. Add to flour mixture; add eggs. Beat with an electric mixer on low speed 30 seconds, scraping bowl. Beat on high speed 3 minutes. Stir in raisins, currants, citron, anise seed, and as much of the remaining flour as you can. On a floured surface, knead in enough remaining flour to make a moderately soft dough that is smooth and elastic (3 to 5 minutes). Place in greased bowl; turn once. Cover and let rise in warm place till double (1½ to 2 hours).

1 **slightly beaten egg**
1 **tablespoon water**

● Punch down. Cover; let rest 10 minutes. Shape into an 8-inch round loaf. Place on a greased baking sheet. Cut a cross ½ inch deep in top. Cover; let rise till *nearly* double (about 45 minutes). Brush with mixture of egg and water. Bake in a 350° oven about 35 minutes or till golden. Makes 1 loaf (16 servings).

Nutrition information per serving: 170 calories, 4 g protein, 30 g carbohydrate, 4 g fat (1 g saturated), 34 mg cholesterol, 125 mg sodium, 93 mg potassium.

RISOTTOS, POLENTAS, & GNOCCHI

In Italy, cooking with grains used to be considered country-style cooking.

Today, however, everyone from rich to poor and young to old has

adopted this cooking style, and wonderful creations

are the outcome. Here you'll discover how to dress up a plain

risotto with a few ingredients, how to serve cornmeal polenta in a

variety of ways, and how to bake extra crispy gnocchi.

Risotto

Arborio rice, which is sold in specialty shops and large supermarkets, makes this Italian specialty extra creamy.

⅓ **cup thinly sliced green onion**
1 **tablespoon margarine *or* butter**
⅔ **cup Arborio *or* long grain rice**

● In a medium saucepan cook the onion in hot margarine or butter till tender but not brown. Add the rice. Cook and stir for 2 minutes more.

2 **cups water**
½ **teaspoon instant chicken bouillon granules**
   Dash pepper

● Carefully stir in the water, chicken bouillon granules, and pepper. Bring to boiling; reduce heat. Cover and simmer for 20 minutes (do not lift cover). Remove from heat.

¼ **cup grated Parmesan or Romano cheese**

● Let stand, covered, for 5 minutes. Rice should be tender but slightly firm, and the mixture should be creamy. (If necessary, stir in a little water to reach desired consistency.) Stir in the Parmesan or Romano cheese. Makes 4 side-dish servings.

Nutrition information per serving: 164 calories, 4 g protein, 26 g carbohydrate, 5 g fat (2 g saturated), 4 mg cholesterol, 242 mg sodium, 57 mg potassium.

Herbed Risotto
1 **tablespoon snipped parsley**
¼ **teaspoon dried basil, crushed**
⅛ **teaspoon dried tarragon, crushed**

Prepare Risotto as directed above, *except* stir the parsley, basil, and tarragon in with the water.

Risotto with Mushrooms
1 **cup sliced fresh mushrooms**
2 **tablespoons dry white wine**

Prepare Risotto as directed above, *except* cook mushrooms with the onion and stir the white wine into the rice with the Parmesan cheese.

Nutrition information per serving: 173 calories, 5 g protein, 27 g carbohydrate, 5 g fat (2 g saturated), 4 mg cholesterol, 243 mg sodium, 126 mg potassium.

Country-Style Risotto
3 **tablespoons finely chopped prosciutto *or* fully cooked ham**
¼ **teaspoon instant chicken bouillon granules**

Prepare Risotto as directed above, *except* cook the prosciutto or ham with the onion and use the ¼ teaspoon chicken bouillon granules.

Nutrition information per serving: 174 calories, 6 g protein, 26 g carbohydrate, 5 g fat (2 g saturated), 8 mg cholesterol, 273 mg sodium, 78 mg potassium.

Risotto Primavera

Add some extra color and flavor to your menu by serving this delicately seasoned combo of rice and fresh vegetables.

¼ cup thinly sliced shallots *or* green onions
2 tablespoons chopped green *or* sweet red pepper
2 tablespoons margarine *or* butter
½ cup Arborio *or* long grain rice

● In a medium saucepan cook shallots or green onions and green or red pepper in hot margarine or butter till vegetables are tender. Add rice. Cook and stir for 2 minutes more.

1¾ cups water
⅓ cup fresh *or* frozen peas
3 tablespoons thinly sliced celery
2 tablespoons shredded carrot
½ teaspoon instant chicken bouillon granules
Dash pepper

● Carefully stir in the water, peas, celery, carrot, chicken bouillon granules, and pepper. Bring to boiling; reduce heat. Cover and simmer for 20 minutes (do not lift cover). Remove from heat.

⅓ cup peeled, seeded, and chopped ripe fresh tomato
⅓ cup quartered fresh mushrooms
¼ teaspoon dried basil, crushed

● Stir in tomato, mushrooms, and basil. Cover and let stand for 5 minutes. Makes 4 side-dish servings.

Nutrition information per serving: 162 calories, 3 g protein, 24 g carbohydrate, 6 g fat (1 g saturated), 0 mg cholesterol, 190 mg sodium, 182 mg potassium.

Rice and Peas

An Italian tradition—rice and peas that are extra creamy.

3 slices bacon
½ cup Arborio *or* long grain rice
2 tablespoons sliced green onion

● In a medium saucepan cook bacon till crisp. Drain bacon, reserving 1 tablespoon drippings. Crumble bacon and set aside. Cook rice and green onion in reserved bacon drippings over medium heat about 2 minutes or till rice is lightly browned.

2 cups water
1 cup fresh *or* frozen peas
1 teaspoon instant chicken bouillon granules
Dash pepper

● Carefully stir in the water, peas, chicken bouillon granules, pepper, and crumbled bacon. Bring to boiling; reduce heat. Cover and simmer for 20 minutes (do not lift cover). Remove from heat.

¼ cup grated Parmesan *or* Romano cheese
2 tablespoons snipped parsley

● Stir in the Parmesan cheese and parsley. Cover and let stand for 5 minutes. Makes 4 side-dish servings.

Nutrition information per serving: 203 calories, 7 g protein, 26 g carbohydrate, 8 g fat (3 g saturated), 29 mg cholesterol, 433 mg sodium, 177 mg potassium.

Polenta

Choose butter, honey, maple syrup, cheese, or a tomato sauce to serve over this warm dish.

3 cups water
1 cup cornmeal
1 cup cold water
1 teaspoon salt

● In a medium saucepan bring the 3 cups water to boiling. In a mixing bowl combine the cornmeal, 1 cup cold water, and salt. Slowly add cornmeal mixture to boiling water, stirring constantly. Cook and stir till mixture returns to boiling. Reduce heat to very low. Cover and simmer for 15 minutes, stirring occasionally. Serve immediately. Makes 6 side-dish servings.

Nutrition information per serving: 84 calories, 2 g protein, 18 g carbohydrate, 0 g fat (0 g saturated), 0 mg cholesterol, 355 mg sodium, 28 mg potassium.

Baked Polenta

Prepare Polenta as directed above, *except* turn the hot mixture into a 9-inch pie plate. Cool for 1 hour. Cover with foil and chill for several hours or overnight till firm. Bake, covered, in a 350° oven about 25 minutes or till heated through. Cut into wedges.

Fried Polenta
2 tablespoons margarine *or* butter

Prepare Polenta as directed above, *except* turn the hot mixture into an 8x4x2- or 9x5x3-inch loaf pan. Cool for 1 hour. Then cover and chill for several hours or overnight till firm. Turn out and cut into ½-inch-thick slices. In a large skillet cook the slices in hot margarine or butter over medium-low heat for 10 to 12 minutes on *each* side or till browned and crisp.

Nutrition information per serving: 118 calories, 2 g protein, 18 g carbohydrate, 4 g fat (1 g saturated), 0 mg cholesterol, 400 mg sodium, 30 mg potassium.

Broiled Polenta
3 tablespoons margarine or butter, melted

Prepare Polenta as directed above, *except* turn the hot mixture into an 8x4x2- or 9x5x3-inch loaf pan. Cool for 1 hour. Then cover and chill for several hours or overnight till firm. Turn out and cut into ½-inch-thick slices. Place slices on the greased, unheated rack of a broiler pan. Brush with some of the margarine. Broil 4 to 5 inches from heat for 8 minutes. Turn slices; brush with remaining margarine. Broil about 8 minutes more or till browned and crisp.

Nutrition information per serving: 135 calories, 2 g protein, 18 g carbohydrate, 6 g fat (1 g saturated), 0 mg cholesterol, 422 mg sodium, 31 mg potassium.

Cheesy Polenta

Chunky Vegetable Sauce
(see recipe, page 10)

Cheesy Polenta

Savor this polenta layered with three kinds of cheese and topped with a thick vegetable sauce.

1 cup shredded mozzarella cheese (4 ounces)
1 cup shredded fontina *or* Gouda cheese (4 ounces)
½ cup grated Parmesan *or* Romano cheese

● In a medium mixing bowl stir together mozzarella cheese, fontina or Gouda cheese, and Parmesan or Romano cheese. Set aside.

Polenta (see recipe, page 93)

● Prepare Polenta as directed, *except* turn a third of the hot mixture into an 8x8x2-inch baking dish. Sprinkle with *half* the cheese mixture. Repeat layers, then top with remaining polenta mixture. Cool for 1 hour. Cover with foil and chill several hours or overnight till firm.
  Bake in a 350° oven about 35 minutes or till lightly browned and heated through. Let stand 10 minutes before cutting.

2 cups Chunky Vegetable Sauce (see recipe, page 10)
Parmesan cheese (optional)

● Meanwhile, in a medium saucepan heat sauce. Serve sauce over polenta portions. If desired, sprinkle with Parmesan cheese. Makes 6 main-dish or 9 side-dish servings.

Nutrition information per serving: 301 calories, 15 g protein, 27 g carbohydrate, 15 g fat (7 g saturated), 38 mg cholesterol, 731 mg sodium, 351 mg potassium.

Cheesy Polenta with Eggs
4 eggs
2 tablespoons milk
Dash salt
Dash pepper
1 tablespoon margarine *or* butter

Prepare Cheesy Polenta as directed above. While polenta is standing for 10 minutes before cutting, beat together the eggs, milk, salt, and pepper. In a medium skillet melt margarine or butter over medium heat; pour in egg mixture. Cook, without stirring, till mixture begins to set on the bottom and around edge.
  Using a large spoon or spatula, lift and fold partially cooked eggs so uncooked portion flows underneath. Continue cooking and folding over medium heat about 2 minutes or till eggs are cooked throughout but are still glossy and moist. Serve eggs over polenta portions, then top with sauce.

Nutrition information per serving: 370 calories, 20 g protein, 27 g carbohydrate, 20 g fat (9 g saturated), 180 mg cholesterol, 819 mg sodium, 360 mg potassium.

Polenta with Sausage

1 pound Italian sausage links, cut into 1½-inch pieces
1½ cups sliced fresh mushrooms
½ cup chopped onion
¼ cup chopped green pepper

● In a large skillet cook the sausage about 10 minutes or till browned. Drain well. Set aside. In the same skillet combine the mushrooms, onion, and green pepper. Cook and stir till vegetables are tender.

1 16-ounce can tomatoes, cut up, *or* 3 medium ripe fresh tomatoes, peeled and chopped
½ cup water
1 bay leaf
¼ teaspoon dried oregano, crushed
¼ teaspoon pepper

● Carefully stir in the *undrained* or fresh tomatoes, water, bay leaf, oregano, pepper, and sausage. Bring to boiling; reduce heat. Boil gently, uncovered, for 30 minutes, stirring occasionally. Discard bay leaf.

¼ cup water
1½ teaspoons cornstarch
Polenta (see recipe, page 93)

● Combine water and cornstarch. Stir into tomato mixture. Cook and stir till slightly thickened and bubbly. Cook and stir for 2 minutes more. Serve sauce over desired form of Polenta. Makes 4 main-dish servings.

Nutrition information per serving: 441 calories, 22 g protein, 37 g carbohydrate, 23 g fat (8 g saturated), 66 mg cholesterol, 1,504 mg sodium, 694 mg potassium.

Country Dinner

In many areas of Northern Italy, rice is as important a staple as pasta. Italian cooks use rice in an array of dishes ranging from entrées to desserts. A favorite and versatile side dish based on rice is risotto *(ree ZOE toe)*.

Its mild flavor and creamy texture make risotto a wonderful complement to any meal. Here you'll find it served with another typical dish from Northern Italy—veal chops with a cream-based caper sauce.

Menu

Veal Chops with Caper Sauce

(see recipe, page 34)

Risotto

(see recipe, page 91)

Italian green beans

Hard rolls

Crostata

(see recipe, page 116)

Crispy Gnocchi

Baking the gnocchi (NAH key) makes it extra crisp. (Pictured on page 46.)

1½ cups milk **2 tablespoons margarine *or* butter**	● In a medium saucepan bring the milk and margarine or butter to boiling.
¾ cup milk **½ cup semolina *or* quick-cooking farina**	● Meanwhile, in a medium mixing bowl stir together the milk and semolina or farina. Slowly add the semolina mixture to the boiling milk, stirring constantly. Cook and stir for 3 to 4 minutes or till thick.
1 beaten egg **⅓ cup grated Parmesan cheese**	● Remove from heat. Stir about *½ cup* of the hot mixture into the egg. Return all to the saucepan. Stir in the Parmesan cheese. Pour into a well-buttered 10x6x2-inch baking dish. Cover and chill about 1 hour or till firm.
2 tablespoons grated Parmesan cheese	● Turn out of baking dish onto a cutting board. Cut into twenty 3x1-inch rectangles. Sprinkle tops with Parmesan cheese. Place on a well-greased baking sheet. Bake in a 425° oven for 20 to 25 minutes or till golden. Serve warm. Makes 5 side-dish servings.

Nutrition information per serving: 179 calories, 9 g protein, 13 g carbohydrate, 10 g fat (4 g saturated), 58 mg cholesterol, 259 mg sodium, 194 mg potassium.

Herb-Garlic Gnocchi **1 teaspoon dried basil, oregano, *or* marjoram, crushed** **⅛ teaspoon garlic powder**	Prepare Crispy Gnocchi as directed above, *except* stir basil, oregano, or marjoram and garlic powder in with the semolina.
Spinach Gnocchi **1¼ cups milk** **1 10-ounce package frozen chopped spinach**	Prepare Crispy Gnocchi as directed above, *except* bring the 1¼ cups milk to boiling with the margarine. Cook spinach according to package directions. Drain in a colander, pressing out as much liquid as possible with a spoon. Stir spinach into hot semolina mixture with the ⅓ cup Parmesan cheese.

Nutrition information per serving: 189 calories, 10 g protein, 16 g carbohydrate, 10 g fat (4 g saturated), 57 mg cholesterol, 301 mg sodium, 344 mg potassium.

ANTIPASTI & SALADS

If you're in need of an appetizer, snack, or salad, look no further.

We've combined favorite Italian ingredients, including pastas,

cheeses, meats, vegetables, and more, to give you an

array of tantalizing recipes. You'll find most of these dishes are

interchangeable—serve them either as an antipasto or a salad.

Fried Cheese Sticks

Dunk the warm cheese sticks into spaghetti sauce for an appetizer or snack.

8 ounces mozzarella *or* fontina cheese

● Cut cheese into 2½x½x½-inch sticks.

2 tablespoons all-purpose flour
1 beaten egg
½ cup fine dry Italian seasoned bread crumbs

● Roll cheese sticks in flour to coat. Then, dip in beaten egg and roll in bread crumbs, making sure cheese is completely coated with crumbs. Chill for 2 to 4 hours or till coating is set.

Cooking oil *or* shortening for deep-fat frying
Purchased spaghetti sauce (optional)

● In a heavy saucepan or a deep-fat fryer, heat 2 inches of cooking oil or melted shortening to 375°. Fry cheese sticks, a few at a time, for 30 to 45 seconds or till golden. Drain sticks on paper towels. Keep them warm in a 300° oven while frying remaining sticks.
  If desired, heat spaghetti sauce and serve with warm cheese sticks. Makes about 20.

Nutrition information per cheese stick: 65 calories, 4 g protein, 3 g carbohydrate, 4 g fat (2 g saturated), 17 mg cholesterol, 74 mg sodium, 15 mg potassium.

Caponata

Serve this tangy eggplant-tomato combo as an appetizer or as a relish with poultry and pork.

1 medium eggplant, peeled and cut into ½-inch cubes (about 4 cups)
¾ cup chopped onion
⅓ cup chopped celery
¼ cup olive oil *or* cooking oil

● In a large skillet cook eggplant, onion, and celery in hot olive oil or cooking oil, covered, over medium heat for 5 to 8 minutes or till just tender.

1 16-ounce can tomatoes, drained and cut up
3 tablespoons wine vinegar
2 tablespoons tomato paste
1 teaspoon sugar
½ teaspoon salt
Dash ground red pepper

● Stir in tomatoes, wine vinegar, tomato paste, sugar, salt, and red pepper. Cook, uncovered, over low heat for 5 minutes, stirring occasionally. Remove from the heat.

½ cup sliced pitted ripe olives
2 tablespoons pine nuts
1 tablespoon snipped parsley
1 tablespoon capers, drained

● Stir in olives, pine nuts, parsley, and capers. Cool. Cover and chill for 2 to 24 hours. Let stand at room temperature for 30 minutes before serving. Makes 8 to 10 servings.

Nutrition information per serving: 119 calories, 2 g protein, 9 g carbohydrate, 10 g fat (1 g saturated), 0 mg cholesterol, 293 mg sodium, 302 mg potassium.

Peperonata
(see recipe, page 104)

Marinated Mozzarella

Marinated Mozzarella

8 ounces mozzarella *or* fontina cheese
½ of a medium green *or* sweet red
pepper, cut into ¾-inch pieces
½ cup almond-stuffed olives

● Cut cheese into ½-inch cubes. In a 1-quart container with a tight-fitting lid, place mozzarella or fontina cheese, green or red pepper, and olives. Set aside.

⅓ cup olive oil
⅓ cup white wine vinegar
1 teaspoon dried oregano, crushed
1 teaspoon crushed red pepper
½ teaspoon dried thyme, crushed
1 clove garlic, quartered

● In a small saucepan combine olive oil, vinegar, oregano, red pepper, thyme, and garlic. Cook and stir just till heated through. Remove from the heat; cool to room temperature. Pour over cheese mixture; stir to coat. Cover and marinate in the refrigerator for 1 to 3 days.

To serve, let stand at room temperature about 30 minutes. Drain and discard garlic. Makes 10 servings.

Nutrition information per serving: 149 calories, 6 g protein, 2 g carbohydrate, 14 g fat (4 g saturated), 13 mg cholesterol, 310 mg sodium, 64 mg potassium.

Creating an Antipasto Tray

Antipasto means "before the meal," so this course should only tease the appetite and not be too filling. With the luscious assortment of foods on an antipasto tray, it's often tempting to overindulge. One way to control this is to serve a small antipasto tray. However, a larger antipasto platter makes a wonderful light lunch for a warm summer day or a late supper after the theater or game.

Making an appealing antipasto doesn't require a lot of time or artistic ability. Most of the foods need little preparation—simple foods from the delicatessen or off the shelf are great for an antipasto.

To assemble an antipasto tray, start with a variety of cold cuts, such as salami and ham. Add cheese cubes or slices, green olives, ripe olives, pickled peppers, marinated artichoke hearts, fresh vegetable sticks, and perhaps a relish dish.

For a sweet fruit to complement the flavors of the savory foods, try cantaloupe balls, honeydew melon balls, strawberries, and figs. Make them extra special by wrapping a strip of prosciutto or thinly sliced ham around each piece of fruit. Serve them in a melon shell, as pictured *opposite,* if desired.

To round out the antipasto course, include a crusty bread, breadsticks, or crackers, and wine or sparkling water.

Provolone-Stuffed Mushrooms

24 **large fresh mushrooms, 1½ to**
   2 inches in diameter (about
   2 pounds)

● Wash and drain mushrooms. Remove stems. Set caps aside. Chop enough of the stems to make *2 cups.*

¼ **cup finely chopped onion**
2 **tablespoons chopped green *or* sweet**
   red pepper
1 **clove garlic, minced**
½ **teaspoon dried oregano *or* basil,**
   crushed
2 **tablespoons margarine *or* butter**
¾ **cup shredded provolone *or* fontina**
   cheese (3 ounces)
¼ **cup fine dry bread crumbs**

● In a medium saucepan cook chopped stems, onion, green or red pepper, garlic, and oregano or basil in margarine for 4 to 5 minutes or till tender, stirring often. Remove from heat.

Stir in the cheese and bread crumbs. Spoon about *1 tablespoon* of the crumb mixture into *each* mushroom cap, pressing lightly. Arrange mushrooms in a 15x10x1-inch baking pan.

Bake, uncovered, in a 425° oven for 8 to 10 minutes or till mushrooms are heated through. Serve warm. Makes 24.

Nutrition information per stuffed mushroom: 35 calories, 2 g protein, 3 g carbohydrate, 2 g fat (1 g saturated), 3 mg cholesterol, 51 mg sodium, 152 mg potassium.

Pepperoni-Stuffed Mushrooms
2 **tablespoons fine dry bread crumbs**
⅓ **cup finely chopped pepperoni**

Prepare Provolone-Stuffed Mushrooms as directed above, *except* omit the cheese and use the 2 tablespoons bread crumbs. Stir pepperoni into crumb mixture.

Nutrition information per stuffed mushroom: 35 calories, 1 g protein, 2 g carbohydrate, 2 g fat (1 g saturated), 1 mg cholesterol, 73 mg sodium, 156 mg potassium.

Selecting Olive Oil

Selecting an olive oil, like selecting a wine, is a matter of personal preference. These brief descriptions will guide you in selecting an oil that satisfies your taste and complements the ingredients in the recipe.

Extra virgin olive oil has a zesty olive flavor, strong aroma, and green-gold color.

Virgin olive oil is slightly lighter in flavor and color than extra virgin oil. Both extra virgin and virgin oils are excellent with foods that complement the flavor of the oil, for instance, with fresh vegetables, uncooked dishes, or broiled meats.

Pure olive oil is milder and mellower than the virgin oils. Its flavor is good for pesto, pasta, and salad dressings. Pure olive oil is good for frying or stir-frying because it doesn't smoke easily.

Extra light olive oil is available in some markets. The extra light refers to the flavor, which is delicate like vegetable oil.

To store olive oil, tightly cover the container after each use. Then, place it in a *dark,* cool cupboard. Olive oil will stay fresh for one year.

Baked Cheese

Want a quick appetizer? Here's an impressive dish that's a snap to make.

½ cup **Fresh Tomato and Basil Sauce (see recipe, page 5)** *or* **purchased garden-style spaghetti sauce**
6 ounces **chèvre cheese**
1 teaspoon **lemon juice**
¼ teaspoon **cracked pepper**

● Pour sauce into a 10- or 12-ounce ovenproof baking dish. Using a pastry brush, brush cheese with lemon juice. Sprinkle with cracked pepper. Place cheese atop sauce in the dish. Bake, uncovered, in a 375° oven for 6 to 8 minutes or till cheese is just heated and softened.

6 **hard rolls, sliced,** *or* **melba toast**

● To serve, spread warm cheese and sauce on sliced rolls or melba toast. Makes 6 servings.

Nutrition information per serving: 274 calories, 12 g protein, 32 g carbohydrate, 11 g fat (1 g saturated), 28 mg cholesterol, 455 mg sodium, 97 mg potassium.

Tortellini Toss

8 ounces **packaged cheese tortellini (2 cups)**

● Cook tortellini (see chart, page 8). Drain well. Rinse with *cold* water; drain again.

2 medium **carrots cut into 1½-inch-long julienne strips (about ⅔ cup)**
½ of a **green** *or* **sweet red pepper, cut into 1½-inch-long julienne strips (about ½ cup)**
⅓ cup **Pesto (see recipe, page 16)**
2 tablespoons **grated Parmesan cheese**
2 tablespoons **olive oil**
4 teaspoons **lemon juice**

● In a large bowl combine tortellini, carrot strips, pepper strips, Pesto, Parmesan cheese, olive oil, and lemon juice. Toss till coated. Cover and chill 4 to 24 hours. Let stand at room temperature 30 minutes before serving. Makes 4 to 6 servings.

Nutrition information per serving: 383 calories, 16 g protein, 39 g carbohydrate, 19 g fat (3 g saturated), 50 mg cholesterol, 522 mg sodium, 339 mg potassium.

Peperonata

Doubles as a salad or the centerpiece of an antipasto tray. (Pictured on page 100.)

2 medium sweet red *and/or* yellow peppers
1 medium green pepper

● Halve all of the peppers; remove stems, seeds, and membranes. Place peppers, cut side down, on a foil-lined baking sheet. Bake in a 425° oven for 20 to 25 minutes or till skin is bubbly and browned.

Place peppers in a *new* brown paper bag; seal and let stand for 20 to 30 minutes or till cool enough to handle.

Peel skin from peppers. Cut peppers lengthwise into ½-inch-wide strips, then cut strips crosswise in half. Set aside.

1 small onion, thinly sliced and separated into rings
2 cloves garlic, minced
1 tablespoon snipped fresh oregano *or* 1 teaspoon dried oregano, crushed
½ teaspoon salt
1 tablespoon olive oil
1 tablespoon margarine *or* butter

● In a large skillet cook and stir onion, garlic, oregano, and salt in olive oil and margarine or butter till onion is tender.

2 medium ripe fresh tomatoes, peeled, seeded, and coarsely chopped
2 tablespoons snipped parsley

● Stir in pepper strips and tomatoes. Transfer mixture to a serving bowl. Cover and chill well.

Before serving, let stand at room temperature about 30 minutes. Sprinkle with parsley. Makes 8 servings.

Nutrition information per serving: 43 calories, 1 g protein, 3 g carbohydrate, 3 g fat (1 g saturated), 0 mg cholesterol, 154 mg sodium, 120 mg potassium.

Let the peppers stand until they are cool enough to handle easily. Using a paring knife, start at the stem end, then pull the skin off gently and slowly.

Italian Salad with Vinaigrette

2 ounces pepperoni, salami, *or* mortadella
½ cup canned garbanzo beans
4 cups torn salad greens (iceberg lettuce, leaf lettuce, curly endive, escarole, romaine)
½ cup shredded mozzarella, provolone, *or* fontina cheese (2 ounces)

● Using pepperoni, salami, or mortadella, chop or cut into strips. Rinse and drain the garbanzo beans. Place the salad greens in a large salad bowl. Add the pepperoni, salami, or mortadella; garbanzo beans; and shredded mozzarella, provolone, or fontina cheese. Toss gently.

Italian Vinaigrette
4 mild pepperonicini *or* other Italian pickled peppers (optional)

● Drizzle Italian Vinaigrette over salad mixture. Toss till greens are well coated. If desired, add pepperonicini or peppers. Makes 4 servings.

Nutrition information per serving: 250 calories, 10 g protein, 8 g carbohydrate, 20 g fat (6 g saturated), 15 mg cholesterol, 428 mg sodium, 221 mg potassium.

Italian Vinaigrette
3 tablespoons olive oil *or* cooking oil
2 tablespoons wine vinegar
2 tablespoons grated Parmesan *or* Romano cheese
½ teaspoon Dijon-style mustard
Dash garlic powder

In a screw-top jar combine olive oil or cooking oil, wine vinegar, Parmesan or Romano cheese, mustard, garlic powder, and ⅛ teaspoon *pepper*. Cover and shake well.

Marinated Vegetable Salad

This salad features the colors of the Italian flag—red, green, and white. (Pictured on page 57.)

3 medium ripe fresh tomatoes
1 medium green pepper
1 small onion
1 medium cucumber, thinly sliced
2 tablespoons snipped parsley

● Cut tomatoes into wedges. Cut green pepper into small squares. Thinly slice onion and separate into rings. In a large bowl combine tomatoes, green pepper, onion rings, cucumber, and parsley.

¼ cup olive oil
2 tablespoons white wine vinegar
1 tablespoon snipped fresh thyme *or* basil *or* 1 teaspoon dried thyme *or* basil, crushed
1 clove garlic, minced

● For dressing, in a screw-top jar combine olive oil, white wine vinegar, thyme or basil, and garlic. Cover and shake well. Pour dressing over vegetable mixture. Toss lightly to coat.

Let stand at room temperature for 1 to 2 hours, stirring occasionally. (*Or,* refrigerate for 4 to 24 hours. Before serving, let stand at room temperature about 30 minutes.) Serves 6 to 8.

Nutrition information per serving: 106 calories, 1 g protein, 6 g carbohydrate, 9 g fat (1 g saturated), 0 mg cholesterol, 7 mg sodium, 256 mg potassium.

105

Vegetable Platter with Vinaigrette

2 small ripe fresh tomatoes, sliced
1 small cucumber, thinly sliced
2 hard-cooked eggs, sliced
1 small carrot

● On a serving plate arrange tomatoes around the edge. Arrange cucumber slices and then egg slices on the plate, overlapping rows. Using a vegetable peeler, cut carrot into long strips. Place carrot strips in the center of the plate.

2 tablespoons olive oil *or* cooking oil
1 tablespoon white wine vinegar *or* vinegar
¼ teaspoon Dijon-style mustard
⅛ teaspoon garlic powder
⅛ teaspoon dried basil, crushed

● For vinaigrette, in a screw-top jar combine olive oil or cooking oil, vinegar, mustard, garlic powder, and basil. Cover and shake well.
   Just before serving, drizzle vinaigrette over vegetables on the plate. Makes 8 servings.

Nutrition information per serving: 62 calories, 2 g protein, 3 g carbohydrate, 5 g fat (1 g saturated), 53 mg cholesterol, 26 mg sodium, 127 mg potassium.

Marinated Pasta Toss

An easy dish to tote to a potluck dinner.

4 ounces packaged fusilli *or* spaghetti

● Break fusilli or spaghetti in half. Cook pasta (see chart, page 8). Immediately drain. Rinse pasta with *cold* water, and drain again.

1 6-ounce jar marinated artichoke hearts
½ of a small zucchini
½ of a small yellow summer squash
4 ounces thinly sliced fully cooked ham *or* salami, cut into strips
1 cup shredded provolone *or* mozzarella cheese (4 ounces)
¼ cup sliced pitted ripe olives
2 tablespoons grated Parmesan cheese

● Drain artichoke hearts, reserving marinade. Cut up artichokes. Cut zucchini and yellow squash lengthwise in half. Then cut into slices.
   In a large bowl combine artichokes, zucchini slices, yellow squash slices, ham or salami, provolone or mozzarella cheese, olives, Parmesan cheese, and pasta. Gently toss.

2 tablespoons olive oil *or* cooking oil
2 tablespoons white wine vinegar
2 cloves garlic, minced
1 teaspoon dried basil, crushed
½ teaspoon dried oregano, crushed
¼ teaspoon pepper
Lettuce leaves

● For dressing, in a screw-top jar combine the reserved artichoke marinade, olive oil or cooking oil, wine vinegar, garlic, basil, oregano, and pepper. Cover and shake well. Pour over salad. Gently toss to coat. Cover and chill for 4 to 24 hours. Serve on lettuce-lined plates. Makes 8 side-dish or 4 main-dish servings.

Nutrition information per serving: 197 calories, 11 g protein, 15 g carbohydrate, 11 g fat (4 g saturated), 19 mg cholesterol, 483 mg sodium, 222 mg potassium.

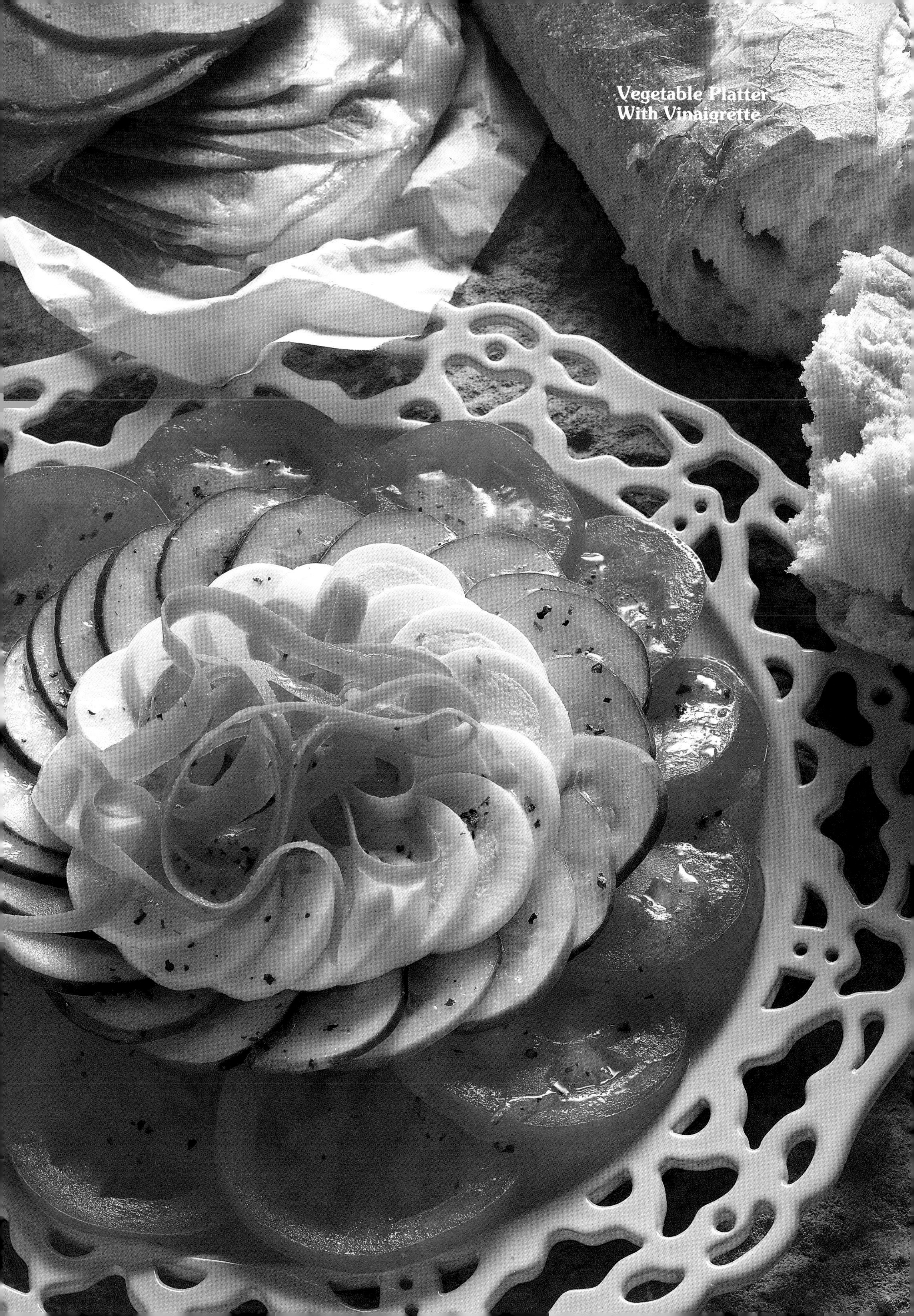
Vegetable Platter With Vinaigrette

VEGETABLES

Fresh vegetables are featured in almost every Italian

meal. Vegetables most often are blended into

sauces, served as an antipasto, or prepared as a side dish. In this

chapter, we offer a sampling of vegetable side dishes

ranging from the simple and elegant Asparagus 'n' Parmesan to the

hearty and homey Fontina- and Rice-Stuffed Peppers.

Asparagus 'n' Parmesan

¾ **pound asparagus spears** *or* **one 10-ounce package frozen asparagus spears**

● For fresh asparagus, snap off and discard woody bases. Cook, covered, in a small amount of boiling water for 8 to 10 minutes or till crisp-tender. (*Or*, cook frozen asparagus according to package directions.) Drain.

2 **tablespoons finely chopped onion**
1 **tablespoon margarine** *or* **butter**
¼ **cup finely shredded Parmesan** *or* **asiago cheese (1 ounce)**

● Meanwhile, in a small saucepan cook onion in margarine or butter till tender but not brown. Drizzle onion mixture over asparagus. Sprinkle with Parmesan or asiago cheese. Serves 4.

Nutrition information per serving: 81 calories, 5 g protein, 4 g carbohydrate, 5 g fat (2 g saturated), 5 mg cholesterol, 168 mg sodium, 280 mg potassium.

Sautéed Carrots

This easy fix-up makes the vegetable the highlight of the meal.

3 **cups thinly bias-sliced carrots**
1 **clove garlic, minced**
1 **tablespoon margarine** *or* **butter**

● In a large skillet cook and stir carrots and garlic in hot margarine or butter for 5 minutes.

½ **cup dry marsala, dry sherry,** *or* **chicken broth**
¼ **teaspoon dried marjoram, crushed**
¼ **teaspoon dried basil, crushed**

● Add marsala, marjoram, and basil. Cook, uncovered, for 5 to 7 minutes or till carrots are crisp-tender, stirring often. Serves 4.

Nutrition information per serving: 115 calories, 1 g protein, 13 g carbohydrate, 3 g fat (1 g saturated), 0 mg cholesterol, 114 mg sodium, 296 mg potassium.

Country-Style Peas

1 **ounce thinly sliced prosciutto** *or* **fully cooked ham**
¼ **cup chopped onion**
1 **tablespoon margarine** *or* **butter**

● Cut prosciutto or ham into thin strips. In a medium saucepan cook prosciutto or ham strips and onion in hot margarine or butter till onion is tender but not brown.

1 **10-ounce package frozen peas**
⅓ **cup torn leaf lettuce**
¼ **cup water**
½ **teaspoon instant chicken bouillon granules**
¼ **teaspoon dried oregano, crushed**
¼ **cup toasted pine nuts** *or* **chopped toasted walnuts**

● Stir in peas, lettuce, water, bouillon granules, oregano, and dash *pepper*. Cover and simmer 4 to 5 minutes or till peas are just tender. Stir in nuts. Serve with a slotted spoon. Serves 4.

Nutrition information per serving: 143 calories, 8 g protein, 12 g carbohydrate, 8 g fat (1 g saturated), 4 mg cholesterol, 303 mg sodium, 219 mg potassium.

Artichokes with Butter Sauce

To eat the artichokes, pluck off a leaf, swirl it in the sauce, then pull the leaf through your teeth, scraping off the tender, nut-flavored flesh at the base of the leaf.

2 medium artichokes (about 10 ounces each)
Lemon juice

● Wash artichokes. Trim stems and remove loose outer leaves. Cut 1 inch from each top. Snip off the sharp leaf tips. Brush cut surfaces with lemon juice. Cut artichokes lengthwise into halves. Brush the cut surfaces with lemon juice.

¾ cup chicken broth

● In a large skillet bring chicken broth to boiling. Carefully add artichoke halves, cut side down. Return to boiling; reduce heat. Cook, covered, over medium-low heat for 20 to 25 minutes or till a leaf pulls out easily. Remove the fuzzy choke from each artichoke half. Transfer artichokes to a serving dish.

2 tablespoons finely chopped onion
⅓ cup margarine *or* butter
2 tablespoons lemon juice
2 teaspoons snipped parsley
½ teaspoon dried tarragon *or* oregano, crushed

● Meanwhile, for sauce, in a small saucepan cook onion in hot margarine or butter till tender but not brown. Stir in lemon juice, parsley, and tarragon or oregano. Serve sauce with artichokes. Makes 4 servings.

Nutrition information per serving: 173 calories, 3 g protein, 8 g carbohydrate, 15 g fat (3 g saturated), 0 mg cholesterol, 362 mg sodium, 234 mg potassium.

Using a small spoon, make a cut just below the fuzzy, thistle portion of the artichoke. Then, scrape out the choke and center leaves; discard.

Eggplant Parmigiana

Serve this flavor-packed dish with a simple baked fish or chicken entrée.

1 small eggplant (about ¾ pound)
1 beaten egg
¼ cup all-purpose flour
2 tablespoons cooking oil

● Peel eggplant and cut crosswise into ½-inch-thick slices. Dip slices into egg, then into flour, turning to coat both sides.

In a large skillet cook eggplant, *half* at a time, in hot cooking oil for 4 to 6 minutes or till golden, turning once. (If necessary, add additional oil.) Drain on paper towels.

⅓ cup grated Parmesan cheese
1 cup Chunky Vegetable Sauce
   (see recipe, page 10) *or* purchased
   garden-style spaghetti sauce
1 cup shredded mozzarella cheese
   (4 ounces)

● Arrange eggplant slices in a single layer in a 12x7½x2-inch baking dish. Sprinkle with Parmesan cheese. Top with sauce and mozzarella cheese. Bake, covered, in a 400° oven 10 to 15 minutes or till hot. Serves 4.

Nutrition information per serving: 277 calories, 14 g protein, 17 g carbohydrate, 18 g fat (6 g saturated), 74 mg cholesterol, 396 mg sodium, 407 mg potassium.

Skillet Eggplant Parmigiana

Prepare Eggplant Parmigiana as directed above, *except* after browning eggplant slices, wipe skillet with paper towels. Arrange eggplant slices in the skillet. Sprinkle with Parmesan cheese. Top with sauce and mozzarella cheese. Cook, covered, over medium-low heat for 5 to 7 minutes or till heated through.

Zesty Green Beans

Strips of salami and tarragon vinegar or wine vinegar add zip to the beans.

1 9-ounce package frozen Italian-style
   green beans

● Cook beans according to package directions. Drain well. Set aside.

⅓ cup sliced green onions
1 clove garlic, minced
1 tablespoon margarine *or* butter
1 ounce salami, cut into thin strips
   (about ¼ cup)
2 tablespoons tarragon vinegar *or* wine
   vinegar
1 tablespoon snipped parsley
   Dash pepper

● Meanwhile, in a small saucepan cook and stir onion and garlic in hot margarine or butter till onion is tender but not brown. Add salami, vinegar, parsley, and pepper. Cook and stir for 1 minute. Stir in beans, and cook till heated through. Makes 4 servings.

Nutrition information per serving: 83 calories, 3 g protein, 7 g carbohydrate, 5 g fat (1 g saturated), 6 mg cholesterol, 166 mg sodium, 201 mg potassium.

Italian-Style Vegetable Stir-Fry

Italian-Style Vegetable Stir-Fry

Snip the herbs and chop all of the vegetables before heating the wok or skillet, then stir-fry this dish in only 5 minutes.

1 **tablespoon cooking oil**
1 **clove garlic, minced**
1 **small zucchini, halved lengthwise and sliced ¼ inch thick (1 cup)**
1 **small yellow summer squash, halved lengthwise and sliced ¼ inch thick (1 cup)**
3 **green onions, bias-sliced into 1-inch lengths**

● Preheat a wok or large skillet over high heat. Add cooking oil. (If necessary, add more oil during cooking.)
　Stir-fry garlic in hot oil for 15 seconds. Add sliced zucchini and yellow squash. Stir-fry for 1½ minutes.
　Add green onions. Stir-fry about 1½ minutes or till vegetables are crisp-tender.

1 **medium ripe fresh tomato, seeded and chopped**
2 **tablespoons snipped parsley**
1 **tablespoon snipped fresh basil *or* ½ teaspoon dried basil, crushed**
¼ **cup finely shredded asiago *or* Parmesan cheese**

● Stir in tomato, parsley, and basil. Cook and stir 1 minute or till heated through. Sprinkle with cheese. Serve immediately. Serves 4.

Nutrition information per serving: 74 calories, 3 g protein, 5 g carbohydrate, 5 g fat (1 g saturated), 4 mg cholesterol, 99 mg sodium, 244 mg potassium.

Fontina- and Rice-Stuffed Peppers

2 **medium green, sweet red, *or* yellow peppers, halved lengthwise**

● Remove stems, seeds, and membranes from peppers. In a saucepan cook peppers, covered, in boiling water for 3 minutes. Drain well.

1 **clove garlic, minced**
1 **tablespoon margarine *or* butter**
1 **tablespoon all-purpose flour**
½ **cup milk**
½ **cup shredded fontina *or* provolone cheese (2 ounces)**
1 **cup cooked long grain rice**
1 **small ripe fresh tomato, peeled, seeded, and chopped**
2 **green onions, thinly sliced**
2 **tablespoons snipped parsley**
½ **teaspoon dried Italian seasoning, crushed**

● For filling, in a small saucepan cook the garlic in hot margarine or butter for 1 minute. Stir in flour. Add milk all at once. Cook and stir till thickened and bubbly. Stir in fontina or provolone cheese. Remove from the heat.
　Stir in rice, tomato, onions, parsley, Italian seasoning, and ⅛ teaspoon *pepper.*

¼ **cup grated Parmesan cheese**

● Place pepper shells in an 8x8x2-inch baking dish. Spoon filling into shells. Sprinkle with cheese. Bake in a 375° oven about 20 minutes or till heated through. Serves 4.

Nutrition information per serving: 311 calories, 11 g protein, 45 g carbohydrate, 10 g fat (5 g saturated), 23 mg cholesterol, 150 mg sodium, 272 mg potassium.

DESSERTS

Although Italians typically end a meal with fresh fruit, cheese, or

a light dessert, they serve more elaborate desserts for special

occasions. Here you'll find a treasury of desserts such as our

country-style baked Crostata, the shortcut classic Zuppa Inglese, and

new pasta desserts including Berry-Chocolate Manicotti. There's

also a special section featuring the popular Italian ice cream, Gelato.

Cannoli

Another time, try this filling in sugar ice-cream cones or over pound cake.

2 cups ricotta cheese **¼ cup sugar** **1 teaspoon vanilla** **¼ cup miniature semisweet chocolate pieces** **1 tablespoon candied orange peel, finely chopped (optional)**	● For filling, in a medium bowl combine ricotta cheese, sugar, and vanilla. Stir or beat till smooth. Fold in chocolate pieces and, if desired, candied orange peel. Cover and chill.
12 purchased cannoli cones **Powdered sugar**	● Spoon filling into a decorating bag fitted with a large tip. Pipe filling into cones. Sift with sugar. Chill up to 1 hour. Serves 12.

Nutrition information per serving: 171 calories, 6 g protein, 18 g carbohydrate, 9 g fat (6 g saturated), 23 mg cholesterol, 95 mg sodium, 64 mg potassium.

Chocolate Cannoli **4 teaspoons unsweetened cocoa powder**	Prepare Cannoli as directed above, *except* omit candied orange peel. Stir cocoa powder into the filling with the sugar.

Berry-Chocolate Manicotti

Stuff manicotti with a ricotta-strawberry filling, and top with chocolate for an elegant dessert.

6 packaged manicotti *or* cannelloni shells	● In a large saucepan cook pasta shells in a large amount of boiling water for 20 minutes. Drain. Rinse with *cold* water; drain well.
1½ cups ricotta cheese **1 3-ounce package cream cheese, softened** **¼ cup sugar** **1 teaspoon vanilla** **1 cup sliced strawberries**	● For filling, in a medium mixing bowl combine ricotta cheese, cream cheese, sugar, and vanilla. Beat with an electric mixer on low to medium speed till creamy. Fold in berries. Using a small spoon, stuff about ½ cup of the filling into *each* cooked shell. (See how-to, page 22.) Chill well or for up to 5 hours.
¼ cup semisweet chocolate pieces **3 tablespoons corn syrup** **¼ cup light cream *or* milk**	● For sauce, in a small heavy saucepan heat chocolate and corn syrup over low heat till chocolate melts, stirring constantly. Gradually stir in cream. Remove from heat. Chill well.
6 large strawberries	● Place filled shells on dessert plates. Drizzle with sauce. Garnish with berries. Serves 6.

Nutrition information per serving: 325 calories, 10 g protein, 35 g carbohydrate, 17 g fat (10 g saturated), 50 mg cholesterol, 104 mg sodium, 203 mg potassium.

Crostata

Pass a pitcher of light cream for a perfect topping to this warm apple tart.

2 cups all-purpose flour
⅓ cup sugar
2 teaspoons baking powder
⅔ cup margarine *or* butter
1 slightly beaten egg
¼ cup milk
1 teaspoon vanilla

● In a medium bowl stir together flour, sugar, and baking powder. Cut in margarine or butter till mixture resembles coarse crumbs.

Combine egg, milk, and vanilla; add to flour mixture. Mix well. On a lightly floured surface knead gently 10 to 12 strokes or till smooth.

Chill *one-third* of the dough. Pat remaining dough onto the bottom and up the sides of a 10-inch tart pan. (*Or,* if desired, use a 10-inch tart pan with a removable bottom.)

4 cups sliced, peeled apples
⅔ cup apricot *or* peach preserves
¼ cup sugar

● Arrange apple slices over pastry in the tart pan. Stir together preserves and sugar. Spread evenly over apples.

Milk
Sugar

● On a lightly floured surface, roll chilled pastry into a 10-inch circle. Cut into ½-inch-wide strips. Arrange strips over apples in a lattice pattern. Trim strips to edges of the pan. Brush lattice with milk. Sprinkle with sugar.

Bake in a 375° oven for 45 to 50 minutes or till fruit is tender. If necessary to prevent overbrowning, cover loosely with foil the last 10 to 15 minutes. If desired, remove tart from the pan. Serve warm. Makes 8 to 10 servings.

Nutrition information per serving: 428 calories, 5 g protein, 66 g carbohydrate, 17 g fat (3 g saturated), 27 mg cholesterol, 268 mg sodium, 138 mg potassium.

Italian Coffee

Since the sixteenth century when coffee was introduced in Venice, Italians have been noted for their love of strong, black coffee. Their espresso has become popular throughout the world as a strong after-dinner coffee.

To brew espresso for your Italian menu, purchase a finely ground, dark roast coffee at the supermarket or a coffee shop. Use an espresso maker, which brews quickly under pressure, to produce coffee with a foamy top. (If you don't have an espresso maker, you can improvise and brew espresso coffee in a drip coffee maker or even use instant espresso coffee crystals.) Espresso is usually served in tiny cups with sugar and a twist of lemon peel.

Cappuccino is another popular Italian coffee. Traditionally, cappuccino is a blend of one-third espresso and two-thirds steamed milk. Instant cappuccino coffee powder is available in supermarkets.

Crostata

Classic Ricotta Cheesecake

Candied orange peel and raisins in the tangy ricotta filling make an irresistible cheesecake.

¾ cup all-purpose flour
3 tablespoons sugar
½ teaspoon finely shredded lemon peel
⅓ cup margarine *or* butter
1 beaten egg yolk

● In a medium bowl stir together flour, sugar, and lemon peel. Cut in margarine or butter till mixture is crumbly. Stir in egg yolk.

Remove the sides from an 8-inch springform pan. Press *one-third* of the dough onto the bottom of the springform pan. Bake in a 350° oven for 7 to 10 minutes or till golden. Cool on a wire rack.

Butter sides of the pan, then attach to the bottom. Press remaining dough 1½ inches up sides of the pan. Set pan aside.

3 cups ricotta cheese
½ cup sugar
¼ cup milk
2 tablespoons all-purpose flour
3 eggs
¼ cup light raisins
2 tablespoons chopped candied orange peel
1 teaspoon finely shredded lemon peel

● In a large mixer bowl beat ricotta cheese, sugar, milk, and flour with an electric mixer till well combined. Add eggs all at once, beating on low speed just till combined. Stir in raisins, candied orange peel, and lemon peel. Pour mixture into the crust-lined pan.

Place the springform pan on a shallow baking pan in the oven. Bake in a 350° oven about 45 minutes or till center appears nearly set when shaken.

Cool 15 minutes. Loosen the sides of the pan. Cool for 30 minutes more; remove sides of the pan. Cool completely. Chill the cheesecake to store. Makes 8 to 10 servings.

Nutrition information per serving: 407 calories, 15 g protein, 37 g carbohydrate, 22 g fat (10 g saturated), 154 mg cholesterol, 196 mg sodium, 167 mg potassium.

Chocolate-Chip Ricotta Cheesecake
½ cup miniature semisweet chocolate pieces

Prepare Classic Ricotta Cheesecake as directed above, *except* substitute chocolate pieces for the raisins and candied orange peel.

Nutrition information per serving: 437 calories, 15 g protein, 37 g carbohydrate, 26 g fat (12 g saturated), 154 mg cholesterol, 196 mg sodium, 165 mg potassium.

Cannoli Cake

Celebrate a birthday, anniversary, or any holiday with this four-layer cake.

3 cups all-purpose flour
2 cups sugar
1 tablespoon baking powder
1½ cups milk
½ cup margarine *or* butter, softened
1½ teaspoons vanilla
2 eggs

● In a large mixing bowl combine the flour, sugar, and baking powder. Add the milk, margarine or butter, and vanilla. Beat with an electric mixer on low speed till combined. Beat on high speed for 2 minutes.

Add eggs and beat 2 minutes more. Pour into 2 greased and floured 9x1½-inch round baking pans.

Bake in a 375° oven for 25 to 30 minutes or till a wooden toothpick inserted near the centers comes out clean. Cool on wire racks for 10 minutes. Remove from pans. Cool thoroughly.

2 cups ricotta cheese
½ cup sugar
1½ teaspoons vanilla
1 teaspoon finely shredded orange peel
½ cup miniature semisweet chocolate pieces
2 tablespoons ground pistachio nuts *or* almonds

● Meanwhile, for filling, in a medium mixing bowl combine the ricotta cheese, sugar, vanilla, and orange peel. Beat with an electric mixer on low to medium speed till creamy. Stir in the chocolate pieces and ground nuts.

● Cut each cake layer in half *horizontally* for a total of 4 layers. (As a cutting guide, insert toothpicks halfway up the sides of each cake layer. Then, use a long-bladed serrated knife to cut through each layer.)

Place 1 cake layer on a cake plate. Spread *⅓ cup* of the filling on the layer. Repeat layers twice. Place remaining cake layer on top of the cake. Set aside.

1 cup shortening
1½ teaspoons vanilla
¼ teaspoon orange *or* almond extract
4½ cups sifted powdered sugar
3 to 4 tablespoons milk

● For frosting, in a large mixing bowl beat shortening, vanilla, and orange or almond extract with an electric mixer on medium speed for 30 seconds. Slowly add *half* of the powdered sugar, beating well. Beat in *2 tablespoons* of the milk.

Gradually beat in remaining powdered sugar and enough remaining milk to make frosting of spreading consistency.

Frost sides and top of the cake. Chill the cake to store. Makes 12 servings.

Nutrition information per serving: 784 calories, 11 g protein, 110 g carbohydrate, 35 g fat (12 g saturated), 59 mg cholesterol, 238 mg sodium, 172 mg potassium.

Zuppa Inglese

Layers of cake, liqueur, and custard create this spectacular dessert.

⅓ **cup sugar**
1 **tablespoon cornstarch**
⅛ **teaspoon salt**
1¼ **cups milk**
1 **beaten egg yolk**
1 **teaspoon vanilla**
1 **square (1 ounce) semisweet
  chocolate, melted**

● For custard, in a medium saucepan stir together sugar, cornstarch, and salt. Stir in the milk. Cook and stir till thickened and bubbly; cook and stir 2 minutes more. Gradually stir *half* of the hot mixture into the egg yolk; return to the pan. Cook and stir till bubbly; cook and stir 2 minutes more. Stir in vanilla.

Pour ⅓ *cup* of the custard into a small bowl. Stir in the melted chocolate. Cover surfaces of chocolate and vanilla custards with plastic wrap. Cool without stirring.

1 **10¾-ounce frozen pound cake,
  thawed and cut into ¼-inch slices**
2 **tablespoons rum**
2 **tablespoons cherry *or* orange liqueur**

● In the bottom of a 1½-quart soufflé dish, arrange *one-fourth* of the cake slices, cutting to fit as necessary. Brush with *half* of the rum.

Spoon *half* of the vanilla custard over cake. Arrange another *fourth* of the cake slices over the custard and brush with *half* of the cherry or orange liqueur. Spoon chocolate custard over cake.

Repeat cake, rum, and vanilla custard layers. Top with remaining cake slices and brush with remaining liqueur. Cover and chill 3 to 4 hours.

½ **cup whipping cream**
1 **tablespoon sugar**
2 **tablespoons sliced *or* slivered
  almonds, toasted**

● Just before serving, whip cream and sugar till stiff peaks form. Spoon or pipe on top of the cake layer. Sprinkle with almonds. Serves 8.

Nutrition information per serving: 314 calories, 5 g protein, 37 g carbohydrate, 16 g fat (9 g saturated), 135 mg cholesterol, 202 mg sodium, 130 mg potassium.

Zabaglione

Whip up this foamy wine custard in about 10 minutes using just four ingredients.

3 **egg yolks**
⅓ **cup dry marsala *or* cream sherry**
¼ **cup sugar**
  Dash salt

● In the top of a double boiler beat egg yolks and marsala or cream sherry till combined. Stir in sugar and salt. Place over *boiling* water (upper pan should not touch the water). Beat with an electric mixer on high speed for 7 to 8 minutes or till mixture thickens and mounds.

Serve immediately in stemmed glasses or over fresh fruit. Makes 4 servings.

Nutrition information per serving: 120 calories, 2 g protein, 14 g carbohydrate, 4 g fat (1 g saturated), 160 mg cholesterol, 39 mg sodium, 29 mg potassium.

Pears with Raspberry Sauce

Cut a thin slice off the bottoms of the pears so they will stand upright in the dessert dishes.

1½ cups dry red wine
¾ cup water
½ cup sugar
2 tablespoons lemon juice
4 medium pears

● In a large saucepan combine wine, water, sugar, and lemon juice. Bring to boiling. Meanwhile, peel and core pears, *leaving stem attached.* Carefully add pears to wine mixture. Return to boiling. Simmer, covered, for 10 to 15 minutes or till pears pierce easily with a fork. Turn pears occasionally for even color. Cool in wine mixture, turning occasionally.

1 10-ounce package frozen raspberries, thawed
¼ cup sugar
1 teaspoon cornstarch
2 tablespoons lemon juice

● Press *undrained* berries through a sieve. Discard seeds. In a small saucepan stir together sugar and cornstarch. Stir in berries and lemon juice. Cook and stir till thickened and bubbly. Cook and stir 2 minutes more. Pour into a bowl. Cover surface with plastic wrap. Chill.

Chocolate leaves (optional)
Sweetened whipped cream

● Drain pears; discard syrup. Place pears in individual dessert dishes; spoon raspberry sauce over pears. If desired, garnish with chocolate leaves. Serve with whipped cream. Serves 4.

Nutrition information per serving: 490 calories, 2 g protein, 86 g carbohydrate, 12 g fat (7 g saturated), 41 mg cholesterol, 19 mg sodium, 429 mg potassium.

Custard and Pasta

2 beaten eggs
1⅓ cups milk *or* light cream
¼ cup sugar
½ teaspoon vanilla *or* 1 tablespoon amaretto, rum, *or* brandy

● For custard, in a heavy medium saucepan combine eggs, milk or light cream, and sugar. Cook and stir over medium heat till mixture just coats a metal spoon. Remove from the heat. Stir in vanilla, amaretto, rum, or brandy.

Quickly cool by placing the saucepan in a sink of *ice* water for 1 to 2 minutes, stirring constantly. Pour custard into a bowl. Cover surface with plastic wrap. Chill well.

¾ cup packaged acini di pepe *or* orzo or rosamarina
¼ cup miniature semisweet chocolate pieces
¼ cup sliced almonds, toasted
1 tablespoon candied orange peel, finely chopped

● Cook pasta (see chart, page 8). Immediately drain. Rinse with *cold* water and drain again.

In a medium bowl stir together cooked pasta, chocolate pieces, almonds, and orange peel. Transfer to individual dessert dishes. Spoon custard over pasta mixture. Makes 4 servings.

Nutrition information per serving: 301 calories, 10 g protein, 42 g carbohydrate, 11 g fat (4 g saturated), 114 mg cholesterol, 76 mg sodium, 206 mg potassium.

121

Gelato Galore

If you're an ice-cream fan, you'll love gelato (jell AH toe). It's a rich, smooth, creamy, frozen custard made from milk, sugar, egg yolks, and a variety of flavorings. With just the right touch of sweetness, gelato lets the flavors of the fruit, nuts, or chocolate come through. Sample these varieties, and you'll see why gelato has been an Italian favorite for centuries.

Banana-Rum Gelato:
Prepare Custard Cream Gelato as directed, *except* omit lemon peel or orange peel. Stir ⅓ cup *rum* into the hot cooked mixture. Stir in 3 ripe *bananas,* mashed (1 cup). Chill and freeze as directed.

Custard Cream Gelato

- **6** cups milk
- **1⅓** cups sugar
- **12** beaten egg yolks
- **1** tablespoon grated lemon *or* orange peel

● In a large saucepan combine *3 cups* of the milk, the sugar, and egg yolks. Cook and stir over medium heat till mixture just coats a metal spoon. Remove from the heat. Stir in remaining milk and the lemon or orange peel.
   Cover the surface with plastic wrap. Refrigerate several hours or overnight till completely chilled. (*Or,* place the saucepan in a sink of *ice* water to chill quickly.)

● Freeze in a 4- or 5-quart ice-cream freezer according to the manufacturer's directions. Makes about 2½ quarts (20 servings).

Nutrition information per serving of Custard Cream, Banana-Rum, Strawberry, or Peach Gelato: 140 calories, 4 g protein, 21 g carbohydrate, 5 g fat (2 g saturated), 134 mg cholesterol, 41 mg sodium, 153 mg potassium.

Nutrition information per serving of Amaretti, Hazelnut, or Double Chocolate Gelato: 202 calories, 5 g protein, 26 g carbohydrate, 9 g fat (3 g saturated), 134 mg cholesterol, 53 mg sodium, 162 mg potassium.

Strawberry Gelato: Prepare Custard Cream Gelato as directed, *except* omit lemon or orange peel. In a blender container or food processor bowl, place 3 cups cut-up *strawberries*. Cover and blend or process till nearly smooth. Stir strawberries and, if desired, several drops of red food coloring into cooked mixture. Chill and freeze as directed.

Amaretti Gelato: Prepare Custard Cream Gelato as directed, *except* omit lemon or orange peel. Stir ¼ cup *amaretto* into hot cooked mixture. Chill completely. Stir 2 cups crumbled *soft macaroons* or coarsely crushed *amaretti cookies* into chilled mixture. Freeze as directed.

Double Chocolate Gelato: Prepare Custard Cream Gelato as directed, *except* omit the lemon or orange peel. Before adding the remaining milk to the hot cooked mixture, stir in 6 squares (6 ounces) melted *semisweet chocolate*. Stir with a wire whisk or beat with a rotary beater till smooth. Stir in remaining milk. Chill completely. Stir in 6 ounces chopped *semisweet chocolate or white baking pieces with cocoa butter* (about 1 cup). Freeze as directed.

Peach Gelato: Prepare Custard Cream Gelato as directed, *except* omit lemon or orange peel. In a blender container or food processor bowl, place 2 cups chopped, peeled, ripe *peaches*. Cover and blend or process till nearly smooth. Stir peaches and 1 cup *peach nectar* into the cooked mixture. Chill and freeze as directed.

Hazelnut Gelato: Prepare Custard Cream Gelato as directed, *except* omit lemon or orange peel. If desired, stir ⅓ cup *hazelnut liqueur* into the hot cooked mixture. Stir in 1 cup chopped *hazelnuts (filberts)*. Chill and freeze as directed.

Amaretti Cookies

Serve these crisp cookies with fresh fruit, custard, ice cream, or fruit ices.

1¼ **cups whole almonds, ground**
 1 **cup sifted powdered sugar**

● Line a cookie sheet with brown paper, parchment paper, or foil. Set aside.
 In a medium bowl stir together ground almonds and powdered sugar. Set aside.

2 **egg whites**
 1 **tablespoon amaretto** *or* ¼ **teaspoon almond extract**
 ½ **teaspoon vanilla**

● In a medium mixing bowl beat egg whites, amaretto or almond extract, and vanilla with an electric mixer on medium speed till stiff peaks form (tips stand straight). Fold in almond mixture about *one-third* at a time.

● Drop almond mixture from a rounded teaspoon 1½ inches apart on the prepared cookie sheet. Bake in a 300° oven for 12 to 15 minutes or till just beginning to brown. Turn oven off and leave door closed. Let cookies dry in the oven for 30 minutes.
 Remove cookies from baking sheet and cool completely on a wire rack. Store in an airtight container for up to 4 days. Makes about 30.

Nutrition information per cookie: 40 calories, 1 g protein, 4 g carbohydrate, 2 g fat (0 g saturated), 0 mg cholesterol, 4 mg sodium, 33 mg potassium.

Lemon Ice

The perfect end to a special meal—sweet, refreshing, and light.

½ **cup sugar**
 ½ **cup boiling water**
 1 **cup cold water**
 ¼ **teaspoon finely grated lemon peel**
 ½ **cup lemon juice**

● Dissolve sugar in boiling water. Add cold water, lemon peel, and lemon juice. Pour into a 9x5x3- or 8x4x2-inch loaf pan.
 Freeze about 4 hours or till icy. Stir lemon mixture. Then, freeze for 1 to 3 hours more or till nearly firm, stirring every 30 minutes. (*Or,* freeze without stirring overnight or till nearly firm. Place lemon ice mixture in a blender container or food processor bowl. Cover and blend or process till fluffy, stopping once or twice to scrape the sides.)

Lemon slices (optional)
 Mint leaves (optional)

● Spoon lemon ice into small stemmed glasses. If desired, garnish with lemon slices and mint leaves. Makes 6 servings.

Nutrition information per serving: 69 calories, 0 g protein, 18 g carbohydrate, 0 g fat (0 g saturated), 0 mg cholesterol, 1 mg sodium, 26 mg potassium.

Index

A-B

Amaretti Cookies, 124
Amaretti Gelato, 123
Antipasti
  Antipasto Kabobs, 103
  Baked Cheese, 103
  Caponata, 99
  Cheesy Hot Sandwich
    Loaf, 74
  Fried Cheese Sticks, 99
  Marinated Mozzarella, 101
  Peperonata, 104
  Pepperoni-Stuffed
    Mushrooms, 102
  Provolone-Stuffed
    Mushrooms, 102
Artichokes with Butter
  Sauce, 110
Asparagus 'n' Parmesan, 109
Baked Cheese, 103
Baked Polenta, 93
Baked Swordfish with
  Fennel, 49
Banana-Rum Gelato, 122
Beef
  Beef and Barley Soup, 82
  Beef Braised in Barolo
    Wine, 33
  Beef-Stuffed Peppers, 31
  Italian Beef Roll, 29

Keep track of your daily nutrition needs by using the information we provide at the end of each recipe. We've analyzed the nutritional content of each recipe serving for you. When a recipe gives an ingredient substitution, we used the first choice in the analysis. If it makes a range of servings (such as 4 to 6), we used the smallest number. Ingredients listed as optional weren't included in the calculations.

Beef *(continued)*
  Italian-Style Pepper Steak, 31
  Meatball Vegetable Soup, 82
  Prosciutto-Stuffed Beef
    Rolls, 36
  Seasoned Roast Lamb, 41
Berry-Chocolate Manicotti, 115
Breads
  Bread Fix-Ups, 86–87
  Breadsticks, 84
  Gorgonzola and Onion Flat
    Bread, 88
  Italian Bread, 84
  Mini Italian Loaves, 84
  Onion-Herb Focaccia, 89
  Panettone, 89
  Parmesan and Onion Flat
    Bread, 88
  Sunflower Nut Italian
    Loaves, 85
Broiled Halibut, 56
Broiled Polenta, 93

C

Cannoli, 115
Cannoli Cake, 119
Caponata, 99
Cheese
  Baked Cheese, 103
  Cheese-Stuffed Chicken
    Breasts, 45
  Cheesy Hot Sandwich
    Loaf, 74
  Cheesy Manicotti, 22
  Cheesy Polenta, 95
  Cheesy Polenta with Eggs, 95
  Cheesy Sausage Meat
    Loaf, 32
Chicken
  Cheese-Stuffed Chicken
    Breasts, 45
  Chicken and Tortellini
    Soup, 79
  Chicken Cacciatore, 43
  Chicken Lasagna Rolls, 23
  Chicken Livers with Sage, 47
  Italian Fried Chicken, 44
  Italian Oven-Fried
    Chicken, 44
  Lemon-Herb Chicken, 43
  Pepper-Stuffed Chicken
    Rolls, 42

Chicken *(continued)*
  Primavera Pasta Pie, 18
  Skillet Chicken and
    Vegetables, 47
Chocolate Cannoli, 115
Chocolate-Chip Ricotta
  Cheesecake, 118
Chunky Vegetable Sauce, 10
Classic Ricotta Cheesecake, 118
Classic Spaghetti Sauce, 16
Country-Style Peas, 109
Country-Style Risotto, 91
Creamy Parmesan Pizza
  Sauce, 67
Creamy Tomato Sauce, 11
Creamy White Clam Sauce, 14
Crispy Gnocchi, 97
Crostata, 116
Crumb-Topped Lobster
  Tails, 60
Custard and Pasta, 121
Custard Cream Gelato, 122

D-E

Desserts
  Amaretti Cookies, 124
  Amaretti Gelato, 123
  Banana-Rum Gelato, 122
  Berry-Chocolate
    Manicotti, 115
  Cannoli, 115
  Cannoli Cake, 119
  Chocolate Cannoli, 115
  Chocolate-Chip Ricotta
    Cheesecake, 118
  Classic Ricotta
    Cheesecake, 118
  Crostata, 116
  Custard and Pasta, 121
  Custard Cream Gelato, 122
  Double Chocolate
    Gelato, 123
  Hazelnut Gelato, 123
  Lemon Ice, 124
  Peach Gelato, 123
  Pears with Raspberry
    Sauce, 121
  Strawberry Gelato, 123
  Zabaglione, 120
  Zuppa Inglese, 120
Double Chocolate Gelato, 123
Eggplant Parmigiana, 111

125

Tips

BETTER HOMES AND GARDENS® BOOKS
Editor: Gerald M. Knox
Art Director: Ernest Shelton
Managing Editor: David A. Kirchner
Project Editors: James D. Blume, Marsha Jahns
Project Managers: Liz Anderson, Jennifer Speer Ramundt,
  Angela K. Renkoski

Food and Family Life Editor: Sharyl Heiken
Associate Department Editors: Sandra Granseth,
  Rosemary C. Hutchinson, Elizabeth Woolever
Senior Food Editors: Linda Henry, Mary Jo Plutt, Joyce Trollope
Associate Food Editors: Jennifer Darling, Debra-Ann Duggan,
  Heather M. Hephner, Mary Major, Shelli McConnell
Test Kitchen: Director, Sharon Stilwell; Photo Studio Director,
  Janet Herwig; Home Economists: Lynn Blanchard, Kay Cargill,
  Marilyn Cornelius, Maryellyn Krantz, Jennifer Nuese,
  Marge Steenson, Colleen Weeden

Associate Art Directors: Neoma Thomas, Linda Ford Vermie,
  Randall Yontz
Assistant Art Directors: Lynda Haupert, Harijs Priekulis,
  Tom Wegner
Graphic Designers: Mary Schlueter Bendgen, Michael Burns,
  Mick Schnepf
Art Production: Director, John Berg; Associate, Joe Heuer;
  Office Manager, Michaela Lester

President, Book Group: Jeramy Lanigan
Vice President, Retail Marketing: Jamie L. Martin
Vice President, Administrative Services: Rick Rundall

BETTER HOMES AND GARDENS® MAGAZINE
President, Magazine Group: James A. Autry
Editorial Director: Doris Eby
Food and Nutrition Editor: Nancy Byal

MEREDITH CORPORATION OFFICERS
Chairman of the Executive Committee: E. T. Meredith III
Chairman of the Board: Robert A. Burnett
President and Chief Executive Officer: Jack D. Rehm

COOKING ITALIAN
Editor: Shelli McConnell
Project Manager: Angela K. Renkoski
Contributing Graphic Designer: Lyne Neymeyer
Contributing Editor: Sandra Mosley
Electronic Text Processor: Paula Forest
Food Stylists: Lynn Blanchard, Janet Herwig
Contributing Photographers: Dennis E. Becker, M. Jensen
  Photography

If you would like to order any additional
copies of our books, call 1-800-678-2802
or check with your local bookstore.